When Did You Stop Being You?
In Search Of Your Personal Brand

By

Charlie Seraphin

ANGEL
MOUNTAIN
PUBLISHING

Angel Mountain Publishing, First Edition, September 2021

© Seraphin Media, 2021

All rights reserved. No part of this book may be reproduced or transmitted
in any form or by any electronic or mechanical means, including photocopying, recording
or by any information storage and retrieval system, without the written permission of the
Author, except where permitted by law.

ISBN: 978-1-7377731-0-8

Website: CharlieSeraphin.com

Cover Art: Adobe Stock (Kevin Carden)

Table of Contents

Introduction		1
1.	A Rude Awakening	9
2.	Peace and Quiet	15
3.	Time For Reflection	19
4.	Seeing Yourself	23
5.	Your Name Is Your Brand	33
6.	True Friends	39
7.	Brand Confusion	45
8.	Your Baby Laugh	51
9.	Your Brand Is Your Legacy	57
10.	Simple Tools For Brand Improvement	63
11.	Hitting Bottom	71
12.	Your True Self	75
13.	Everyday People	79
14.	Understanding Your Dreams	87
15.	Think Thoughts Through	91
16.	Be Present	95
17.	Look Into My Eyes	99
18.	Mother Teresa	103
19.	Your Best You	109
Epilogue		113
Acknowledgments		117
About the Author		119

Introduction

Personal branding has become a hot topic these days. There are literally thousands of personal branding "experts" out there now, telling us that we can change our brand simply by projecting a different image. They tell us to carefully curate our social media so that people will see us as we want to be seen.

That's bunk. Common sense tells us that regardless of what image we project, we'll still be who we are.

When most people talk about branding, they really mean advertising. They confuse glamorizing an image with presenting authenticity. They advertise one brand, but in truth, they're somebody completely different in real life. To make matters worse, after a while, they start to believe what they say about themselves.

We like to think of ourselves as self-made. Over time, we have created an image of ourselves, and we work hard to sell that image to the world. We design a story. It's how we want the world to see us, but most times it's not who we are. That stuff you post may be a convenient way to market yourself, but it isn't who you are. Not even close.

So, what constitutes a true personal brand? What are the critical elements?

The concept of personal branding originally grew out of trademarks in the pre-industrial age. Products were made by hand, so artists and craftsmen stamped their work with initials to identify it.

They stood behind what they made and took enough pride in their work to attach their name. A personal brand meant quality and value. It was a mark of pride. Each brand was special and unique.

What most people today call a personal brand just doesn't do justice to the complexity of who we are. Today our online credentials read something like; "I worked here and there. I'm competent at doing this and that." It may say we're a wood carver, but it doesn't demonstrate how good we are. That's not your brand. **Your personal brand is more about values and personal pride than work experience**.

Your personal brand is not an image or a projection. It is better described as the life-spark that precedes your birth and the energy that exists long after you've turned to dust. It's not the color of your skin or the clothes you wear or your job. It's the special things that make you... you. Your brand is made up of the qualities that belong uniquely to you. Just as those artists and craftsmen put their all into their branded products, it's incumbent upon you to always do your best.

Our core values make us unique. They distinguish us and represent the essence of our personal brand. In a sense, your brand is what you hold close in your heart; in essence, your trademark. Are those the things you're posting? Is that how you introduce yourself when you meet someone? Probably not. We're so caught up in image projection that we fail to spend time thinking about what distinguishes our brand: who we are.

When you are in harmony with your personal brand, it's easier to make friends and influence people. But that's not the reason for learning to be who you are. You have purpose. Your life has meaning. We cling to life not because it is without pain or because it is so much fun. Life is a mission. The mission isn't complete until you fulfill your destiny, and destinies can't be fulfilled until you know who you are.

Life is also about accumulating experiences, and some of them only exist in the natural world. Putting your bare foot into an icy stream is a real experience. It makes you feel alive. Living requires feeling alive. The more you experience, the closer you get to understanding who you are and why you're here. How you express that is your personal brand.

There are many books explaining how to build your brand. Most of them talk about digital profiles and effective use of social media. This isn't one of those books. There are also books that tell you what you have to do to become a better person. This isn't one of those either. I don't know if you need to be better. Only you know that. I don't know what makes you special, but I know that every person is special. It's your job to figure out who you are, why you're special, and whether or not you have some work to do on your brand—before you put it out there.

This book is not about projecting brand images. It's about your real personal brand. Successful consumer branding and successful people have similarities. Value, quality, honesty, trust, reliability, and responsibility are brand anchors. They attach to people as easily as they do to products and services. Even if your profile includes "responsible, reliable and honest," it doesn't begin to demonstrate the complexity of your personal brand. Your authentic brand is based on *all* your core values.

Each chapter prompts different questions. How you phrase and develop your questions is private and personal. Your responses are unique to you, so there are no right or wrong answers. What I believe or how I live my life has nothing to do with your brand. How you express your values and build your brand is entirely up to you. When it comes to reflective exercises, some will work for you, others, not so much.

With effort you can overcome past emotional scars from bad experiences. You can give yourself a fresh start, even if you're in the middle of tough times. I'll show you how to get in touch with your deepest held beliefs. If your brand needs work, this book will help a lot. It's pretty simple: Read the book. Think about what you read. Toss it when you finish or share it with a friend. My guess is, when you read the chapter on friends, you'll want to share…but that's your call.

Your personal brand doesn't have to be what other people say it is. Throughout your life, people have tried to define you—to brand you. Don't you think it's time that you start defining your own brand? You don't have to create or invent anything. All you have to do is get in touch with who you are.

Your personal brand may have been buried under years of judgments, assumptions and pretension. I'm not going to tell you who you are, because I have no idea. You're the only one who really knows. The point is that people get trapped in fake brands. They don't always choose them, but once they're trapped, they play along. Before you know it, life has passed you by and you haven't done anything about being who you're supposed to be or doing what you're destined to do.

Developing your personal brand is challenging. As you learn to observe your thoughts, words, feelings, actions and inactions, in other words; when you start paying attention to who you have become, you can begin to become who you want to be. Your personal brand hasn't changed, but your life experiences change every day. Even if you've experienced horrific things in your life, those experiences don't have to define you.

If you want to accomplish something great and become the person you were meant to be, find the person who has been inside you from the beginning. Distinguish who you are from who the world says you are. You might be comfortable with the role that has been assigned to you. You may not be the person your parents, family, friends, co-workers and acquaintances think you are. You may not be the person you've told people you are.

We all tell lies, hold secrets and know the truth. Sometimes we are ashamed of who we are and what we've done. We're afraid that people will discover our secrets. Living a lie and hiding secrets takes a lot of energy. If you direct that energy back to discovering your true self, I promise you will be much happier.

I am not a doctor or psychologist, counselor or preacher. For half of my career, I was a newsman. For the other half, I was a sales and marketing executive. I taught college classes in sales management, and I've worked with some outstanding branding experts. But this is more than a branding book. I am a spiritual person by nature, naturally empathetic, and I enjoy people. I'm serious but I love to have fun. I read and laugh a lot. My brand also includes many personal flaws and stupid mistakes.

Several years ago, I had a life changing experience. I'll tell you a little about that later, but this book isn't about me. I use a few personal stories to illustrate points, but the book is about how to determine who you are and, if necessary, how to become that person. That includes how we see, package and present ourselves. Branding. I'll help you ask the questions. The rest is up to you.

After I wrote *One Stupid Mistake*, I traveled around the country speaking to diverse audiences. I talked to clubs, business associations, corporations and charitable groups. My speeches always revolved around how and why we make decisions. I loved interacting with each audience. Regardless of demographics or where in the country I was speaking, it always came back to the same basic issue. People can't decide what they want. The most consistent answer is, "I don't know." When you have a clear connection to your values, decisions about where to go and what to do are easier.

If your life is a blur, if your routine is fast-paced with little to remember at the end of a day, if you haven't experienced peace of mind for a while, here's a good place to start. Take a break from the virtual world, read this short, simple little book, and have a heart-to-heart conversation with someone you love. You may not solve all your problems, but you can solve the easy ones today, and with some effort, you'll come up with a plan to take on the rest. At a minimum, next time you update your status, your audience will have a better idea of who you are.

This book is designed to help you discover your brand, to

find what's missing. It's simple and easy, like imagining leaves on the bare branches of a tree. It doesn't involve being perfect. Trees aren't perfect, but each is unique. Nobody's perfect, and nobody is just like you. Being you is about being honest and authentic. Can you do that?

1

A Rude Awakening

Imagine a pitcher of ice water being dumped on your head while you're asleep. That sudden cold would jolt you out of your dream world, wouldn't it? You'd be awake, alert, and probably a bit confused.

That's what I want this book to feel like—a blast of ice-cold, honest-to-goodness truth.

So let's start here: *You are not who you think you are.* Your name, title, hashtag, reputation, experience, success or failure—none of those things define you. The real you is the "you" that existed from the beginning. It's the true essence of your eternal soul, the authentic you. The authentic version of you is what I like to call *your personal brand*. Regardless of whether you die at birth or live to be a hundred, your personal brand has been and will be forever.

That's a shock to the system, isn't it? In today's world, it can be hard to believe that there's a "you" inside you that doesn't have anything to do with clicks, clocks, likes or followers. You're more than a digital footprint. And regardless of how special you are, when your heart stops pumping, your lungs stop breathing, and your mind stops thinking, all that's left are the decisions you made up to this moment. Those decisions—which define your personal brand—exist for eternity.

You and I have different faith structures. We may share some beliefs and disagree on others. My job is not to convince you to believe the way I do. I'm not pitching my spiritual path, but I'm encouraging you to think enough of yourself to find your own.

What does that mean in the context of developing your personal brand? People who live within defined faith structures tend to have an easier time connecting with their personal brand. I think that's because they have context. For believers, God is in his heaven and all's right with the world. But whether you believe or don't believe, it's important to acknowledge that there are forces operating in your life that you can't control and may not have previously considered.

Going to work on your personal brand begins with a wake-up call. You are an important person, and you need to realize that. Your every little thought, word, and action counts. Each one is an opportunity to enhance your brand. Every time you screw up, you tarnish your brand. It's one hundred percent on you. Doesn't matter if anybody else sees or knows. You know, and that's what counts. Start with you at the center and work outward.

At the same time, you need to realize that you are not the *only* important person. Although this book will help you get in touch with "you," remember that we're all part of a bigger whole. You're important, but not the beginning or the end of the universe.

My own wake-up call came a while back when I experienced a series of personal crises. I'd lost my job, and I felt like everyone and everything was turning against me. I was angry, confused, depressed, and fading fast. I pushed people away and sunk deeper and deeper into a self-absorbed world. Fortunately, a friend I trusted suggested a retreat. I ended up spending some time at a monastery. I'd never done anything like this before, but desperate times called for desperate measures.

The abbot and monks were warm and welcoming. They weren't quite sure what to make of me, but they agreed to help and invited me to stay as long as I accepted their terms. The deal was simple: 1) respect the rules of the monastery and 2) everybody works. That meant rising early each day for morning prayer services, breakfast, manual labor, mid-day prayer, lunch, chores, meditation, dinner, evening prayer service, a little reading and early to bed. We didn't have the internet or TV. No frills, no phones, no problem.

You might be thinking, that's crazy. And you are right. If you had told me that I'd be living with monks for seven months, I'd have laughed in your face. But I quickly learned that disciplined structure was exactly what the doctor ordered. My room was small, simple and clean and the meals were basic. There was some social interaction, but most of the time we went about our business in silence.

The monastery is located in New Mexico's beautiful Pecos River Valley, so recreation involves walking the grounds along the riverbank and hiking in the mountains. During our walks we did not speak unless spoken to. We'd nod at one another, but there was little or no chit chat.

Silent meals are an integral part of monastic life. Who says you have to talk while you eat? Non-verbal communication is a lot more natural than you might think. Imagine ten people sitting around a table. Nobody talks. You enjoy dinner. You pass the butter and compliment the chef on the stew with gestures and expressions. No one says a word. At the end of the meal, everyone smiles. You've shared a wonderful human experience without words.

Contrast that experience with our profoundly digital lives today. You'd be surprised how many young people, male and female, have never experienced a date. They've never been in a relationship that wasn't virtual. They are uncomfortable with themselves. They fear rejection or ridicule and withdraw. It's hard for them to make eye contact. Many of them never go outside. They live on their phones and computers. In the virtual world, millions communicate, but most feel isolated.

That's not to say that internet technology is bad. Connecting with friends across the country and around the world is wonderful. The speed and efficiency of communication and information sharing is beneficial. But constant "connectivity" is a major reason some people lose touch with their personal brand. If you allow virtual you to replace real you, it becomes more difficult to find authentic you.

There's a simple cure, but it takes courage. Can you put your phone in another room when you go to bed? Can you put it in a drawer and take regular breaks during the day? At the monastery, telephone signals were few and far between. There was a pay phone at the end of the hall in one of the buildings. It was rarely used and never rang. After a few days, I honestly didn't miss "being connected."

Can you live without your phone? Is it a tool or an addiction?

Managing your life, like riding waves, often requires a surrender to powers that you can't control. My monastic experience didn't answer all my questions, but it taught me how to better manage life's waves. For the most part, my seven months there was a time of quiet, peaceful reflection. While dropping everything to live in the mountains with monks might be a little extreme for you, I encourage you to balance your high speed, technology-centered life with some simple visits to nature.

Make a point occasionally to choose human activity over digital activity. Developing your personal brand requires constant attention to detail. You can't experience those details in a virtual world. Photos and video can evoke powerful emotional responses, but they can't compare to real, person-to-person interaction. It's the difference between imagining a pitcher of ice water, seeing one on a screen, and actually feeling it on your face.

Try to have an honest to goodness talk with another human being—not a text or email, but face-to-face conversation. Make a point of having in-person conversations every day. It doesn't matter who you converse with; just put your device aside long enough to engage another person in attentive dialog that includes eye contact.

Pay attention to the details of the conversation. How much was communicated verbally, and how much did you gain from subtle facial gestures and body language? How do you communicate when you're excited? What makes you most effective in getting your point across? Did you notice that the more interested the other person is in what you have to say, the easier it is for you to communicate what you're feeling?

Active listening is a powerful technique. It requires concentration and a committed effort not only to hear, but to understand what another person is saying. While you are listening, you demonstrate interest with head movement or an expression of interest on your face. Pay attention. Don't let your mind drift, especially to the point where you're focused on what you'll say next. Be an active listener during every conversation.

There's more to communication than words.

Your best you and your personal brand are best developed in the context of society. We need one another. We are biologically designed to be social creatures. We naturally crave social interaction as much as we crave solitude, peace and quiet. Life is a balance. We interact with the world. We venture out and find mates…it's how our species survives. That's hard to accomplish in the virtual world. Try to unplug long enough to connect with other humans. Try to have a minimum of one face-to-face conversation each day, even if it means talking to a stranger. Overcome fear and press forward.

Some governments are recommending social distancing. Keeping us apart, confused and afraid isn't healthy. Like wearing a mask, social distancing is beneficial in creating tribal separation, but it doesn't do anything for personal growth, brand awareness, or authenticity. It's impossible to achieve our full potential in an atmosphere of fear and distrust. Love is the only direction that leads to light.

2

Peace and Quiet

It's natural to dream about the future. When you were a child, you may have thought you knew what you were going to do and who you were going to become. Depending on how and where you were raised, you might have thought you'd be a fireman or an opera singer. Sometimes our childhood dreams come true, but more often than not becoming a movie star or a baseball player is supplanted by the reality of a less glamorous profession.

As adults, it's a good idea to stop from time to time and reflect on our journey so far. Whether we accept the life we're living, or long for something more, it's important to understand who we are—right now, today, at this very moment. Our lives may not be as romantic and adventurous as we envisioned. Few of us can honestly say that about life. But today is a perfect day to take stock of who we really are, what we've actually become, and where we're headed on the rest of life's journey.

Introspection is a wonderful way to get in touch with the person who dreamed our youthful dreams. Don't get nostalgic; you're looking back only for perspective. Push through memories and search for a time when you were your best self. That person from your past can consider becoming the person you were meant to be.

Developing your personal brand is an exercise in honest reflection. In every situation, your outcome is a combination of what you were given and what you do with it. You won't accomplish your goal unless you are paying attention and committed to your success. Explore silence and appreciate peace.

Peace and quiet always go together. In order to find your peace, you must turn down the volume. That means unplugging from the virtual world and every other form of artificial stimulation. Time spent in the virtual realm, combined with the rush of everyday life, is a recipe for chaotic living. Peace requires quiet.

Find a place where you can listen. If you live near the ocean or any other natural setting, it's easy. If you live in an urban area, it may be more of a challenge, but there is a courtyard or park, a terrace, rooftop or balcony that offers a break from the noise of the city. Find that place and focus on its natural beauty.

Have you noticed how many people are out walking or jogging along the beach, on a trail, or through the park with earbuds, listening to music or a podcast? There's a time and place for earbuds and listening to recordings. Music calms the soul. But while the birds are singing and the wind is rustling in the trees, take advantage of being outdoors by listening to natural sounds.

Your life is busy. You have responsibilities and obligations, work and social commitments. But taking time every day, for just five minutes to close your eyes and listen, will pay enormous dividends. The more comfortable you become closing your eyes and being quiet, the easier it will be for you to get in touch with your authentic self. If you can devote as little as five minutes a day, you will witness an amazing transformation.

Monks have a specific listening ritual. They close their eyes and listen for a distant sound, the one that is furthest from their ears. Then they lock in on that sound. Only listen to that one, far away, sound. What is it? Where is it? Can you put it in context? If it's a plane, where is it going? If it's a bird, is it flying toward you or away? What color is it? What else can your mind "see" in that distant sound?

There's a truth that's trying to find you. It's inside you. I have no idea what it is, but I know it's there, and I know it won't connect with you unless and until you find peace…and quiet. Take a few minutes right now. Find a nice spot, set this book aside, close your eyes and listen. Listen with a purpose. What do you hear?

3

Time For Reflection

Getting in touch with the real you isn't brain surgery, but it requires concentration. Reflection is a tool, and closed eyes and deep breathing help put you in a reflective mode.

Close your eyes and take a deep breath. Really. Set the book aside and begin to reflect. Let your mind relax but pay attention to your breath. See where quiet reflection takes you. Come back when you're ready.

***

Welcome back. What did you think about? Write down a word or phrase that describes where your reflection took you.

Once a day, every day, take a reflection break. You don't need an agenda, just a commitment to some quiet time thinking about where you've been, where you are, and where you're going. Your reflection may involve questions or challenges, or it may simply be a time when you let your mind drift from one subject to the next. Thinking is powerful. It's amazing how often we get caught up in the hectic nature of life and forget to think. Sometimes we go an entire day or even a week without any down time for just re-calibrating our brains. Don't judge your thoughts, just be aware of them. Eventually you'll have a journal that tells you a lot about who you are.

Reflection is not conversation or debate. The goal isn't to challenge yourself or second guess your actions. Instead, think of it as a chance to get outside your routine and spend a few minutes just being quiet, restful and reflective. Thinking without an end goal, awareness without words, being present without specific focus are all manifestations of reflection. It's part of a discovery process that leads to your authentic self.

If you are surprised by your reflections, write them down. Observe where your mind wants to take you. Don't analyze. Simply be aware of the voice inside you that is learning to communicate anew. There's no rush. Try to experience quiet reflection every day. Some days are better than others, but every reflective session has benefits.

The more you unplug and reflect, the faster you'll find your way. Open to the possibility that there's a "you" inside that you haven't communicated with recently. This isn't a magic show and there's no hocus pocus. When you unplug and disconnect, your personal brand is more accessible. It's a beautiful thing!

Getting in touch is like running into an old friend. You can never know anyone the way you know yourself. Honest reflection is a pathway to inner peace. That experience doesn't exist online, in the virtual world. Inner peace is the harmony of all your thoughts, words and actions in the real, physical world. When you are in sync, people are drawn to you. They will feel the power of your presence and relate to you in wonderful ways. Be still. Find peace in silence.

Think about how many times during the day you are so wrapped up in what you are doing that you don't consider the consequences. We get on life's treadmill and pound out the miles, but when we step off, we haven't gone anywhere or accomplished anything.

Quiet reflection and conscious awareness have too many benefits to list. Suffice it to say that you are likely to derive benefit in areas that I can't even imagine. You are capable of great things! Do something nice for yourself and take some time to reflect. Do it often. Take a break in the middle of the day. Take a couple minutes before or after a meal, when you first awake or just before you drift off to sleep. The more reflection, the brighter the image. Let your light shine.

Reflection is by definition serious thought or consideration. Try to catch yourself doing things when you're not thinking. If you think about it, engaging in activities without being consciously aware of what you're doing is dangerous. Think before you do. As you bring more awareness to every little aspect of your life, you'll have fewer accidents.

In broadcasting, there's an old saying, "the mic is always hot." That means, when you talk in the vicinity of a microphone, assume it's on. There are historic examples of famous people saying things that they thought were private, only to realize that it was recorded or broadcast. Those are "oh crap" moments.

We've all had "oh crap" moments like this when we say something and then see a hurtful look on another person's face. That's because most of us have the habit of talking without thinking.

We think about what we're going to say, but we often forget to consider the impact our words might have on others.

Reflection is a way to process past experiences and prepare for the future. The more time you spend quietly taking stock of your thoughts, words and actions, the more time you spend considering your values and connecting with them, the easier it will be to avoid "oh crap" situations.

4

Seeing Yourself

When we're newborns, we never think about how we are perceived by others. Our entire world is experiential. We are hungry and cry for food. Sometimes we are wet or cold or frightened. Our world consists entirely of feelings and observations. As we grow, we become fascinated by color, movement, and sound.

As toddlers, we begin to notice how other people react to us. Sometimes they laugh when we do something, so we repeat that behavior to get a laugh. Sometimes they frown or react in negative ways, and we learn to suppress behavior associated with negative feedback.

As time goes on, we become adept at behaving in ways that elicit reactions. Most times we seek approval, but sometimes our desire to be noticed leads to reckless actions that prompt a negative response. Along the way, we lose ourselves. Our personal brand is supplanted by something new, shaped by the world around us.

There's a reason that countless millions of people now exist mostly in the selfie world. They confuse social approval with personal value, impression with reality. When you don't have a firm grasp of who you are, you may be tempted to live for social acceptance. Pretending to be somebody you're not in order to make somebody else happy is a dead end.

The Staples Singers' "Respect Yourself" was a huge hit back in the early 1970's. Here are the exact lyrics: "If you don't respect yourself, ain't nobody gonna give a good kahoot (about you na na naa na na)." In other words, if you don't know who you are, why should anybody care about you?

Imagine that you're a drone, hovering above yourself. As you look down from above, who do you see? Is it the person you always wanted to be, or do you see the product of other people's expectations?

I have a friend, who we'll call Joe, that epitomizes this disconnect. Joe acts like one person when he's at work and another person when he gets home. His neighbors think he's mild-mannered, but his wife and family think he's a tyrant. He's a saint at church and a devil at the neighborhood bar.

So who is Joe, really? It's a hard question to answer—even for Joe himself.

We perceive ourselves differently than others perceive us. There's a disconnect between who we are and the image we project. Trying to identify the root cause of this dilemma was the genesis for this book. I traveled to California, New York City, Ohio, Indiana, Texas and Florida conducting seminars on personal branding and listening to people describe themselves.

I developed a simple identity test. It involves writing down three words or phrases that describe the essence of your brand. For example, some people think of themselves as tall, dark, and handsome. Others use descriptors like clever, smart, or capable.

What are your three words? Take a few minutes right now to write them down. Think about them. You may change your mind, but if you had to decide today, what three words describe you? Only three. It doesn't matter whether you're describing physical characteristics or using ethical or value-oriented words. Just write down three words or phrases and put them in your pocket.

The next part involves asking a close friend, relative, partner or someone who really knows you well, someone you trust, to write down three words or phrases describing you. Having done this hundreds of times, the results follow a predictable pattern. Most people get zero or one match. Some get two. Nobody gets all three.

During one of these personal branding seminars in Ohio, a woman in the back of the room screamed out in the middle of our session. She had texted the exercise to her husband. They'd been married for ten years. She was shocked that he gave three very different descriptive words than she had written.

"I don't understand," she cried. "I thought he knew me better than anyone, and he doesn't know me at all. He didn't even get one!" She was so sure that he would describe her the way she described herself. After all, they were soul partners. Their brains were always in sync...until we put them to the test. No matches. Not even close. They had a lot to talk about when she got home that night.

It's no wonder, and it's not his fault. Most times we see ourselves the way we want to be seen instead of the way we are. Our actions often fail to match our brand. We want people to think of us a certain way, but we're sloppy with our thoughts, words or actions. We're putting something out there that's anything but authentic.

We're not paying attention. We get lazy. We act the way we act because it's the way we've been acting. It's one habit after another. We waste energy pretending to be somebody we're not. Who we are-- becomes a question.

Other participants in the seminars were less dramatic, but you could see disappointment on their faces when they learned that close friends and relatives didn't see them the way they wanted to be seen. It happens every day.

It's one reason divorce rates are so high. People think they know one another and then wake up to find a stranger in their bed. We stop paying attention to one another. It's not so much that someone changed. It has more to do with how much effort goes into being authentic. The further a person drifts from the person they could be, the more likely that we will eventually reject them. We're naturally attracted to harmonious behavior and authenticity. We're put off when people are faking it.

Relationships are difficult to begin with. It takes time to build strong relationship foundations. When you waste time posting personal notes and comments online, you lose the opportunity to improve yourself, and your friends and loved ones also miss their chance. If you don't make a concerted effort to build strong personal relationships, if you don't put in the effort, it's only a matter of time before you "unfriend" one another. When one or both stop trying to be their best, it's likely that someone will throw in the towel.

It's a challenge for two people to be empathetic toward one another, especially when it's obvious that effort is lacking. Sharing space with other humans is even more challenging. With so many moving parts it's easy to miss important messages. Feelings are easily hurt, and if you're not working on your brand, committed to being your best you, one of you is likely to dig a hole and crawl in.

Even when we love one another, great relationships require constant attention. Both of you need time together and time apart to reflect and grow. We require air. Strike a balance between together time and quiet time to work on your brand. Take time to breathe and think and feel and remember. It's as important as a cruise or a spa weekend at a fancy resort. If you and your mate are growing together, no force can separate you.

Social media is the wrong venue for serious personal relationships. Likes and comments designed for public consumption aren't likely to communicate your true self. It's hard to have a personal value exchange online, and even if you do, it lacks the in-person charm that only comes from being in the physical presence of another human being.

You might also consider that the time you spend reading posts and sending emojis would be better spent working on you. Introspective examination of your conscience holds a lot more potential than commenting on what you or your friend had for dinner. When you really get to work on strengthening your personal brand, your odds of relationship success go up exponentially. That means being authentic, and careful that your words and actions represent who you really are.

Your personal brand isn't something you have to rehearse, but depending on how far you've drifted, you may need some time and effort to reconnect with it. It isn't an ideal that you strive to accomplish or a character you saw in a movie or read about online. It isn't where you grew up or went to school or any experience you've had, good or bad. The beauty is, it's hiding in plain sight. The challenge is getting past all the crap that's clouding your vision.

If you know who you are, you can be who you want to be. That's a tricky little statement. Let it sink in. You'll find your brand in the deep recesses of your mind. It's inside you. It's the same "you" that's always been. You are who you were as a child, and likely who you will become again in extreme old age. In order to get in touch today, you need to make a conscious commitment. It starts with reflection.

I often ask students to write a simple creed. Begin with "I believe…" I ask them to fill in all the things that they feel strongly about. Some might be universal, such as "I believe in God." Some may be unique, such as "I believe left-handed people are better spellers." It can be serious, or it can be fun. There are no right or wrong answers. Each of us has things we believe. Now consider whether your beliefs are based on experience or were they suggested by someone else? Is there a difference? Sort them out and boil them down.

When you isolate the things you believe in, you can begin to understand who you are, what you think, and why you act the way you do. All three are intricately related. Just as it's hard to understand people talking through a mask, it's impossible to be authentic when you mask your values and beliefs. Are you ashamed of something you believe?

Take a minute to begin composing *your* beliefs. Identify one or two things that are deeply important to you. What do you believe? What is good? What is evil? The more beliefs you can identify as your core beliefs, the closer you are to your brand identity. The point of the exercise is not to convince people to believe what we believe, but to build a personal action plan.

When you identify your beliefs it's time to ask: What am I doing about it? Are my actions in harmony with my belief structure? For example, if I believe that all people deserve equal treatment, but I consistently put a certain group of people down, that's a problem. Your beliefs must be consistent with who you are and what you do. They don't have to conform to published norms, but they must reflect the authentic you.

Don't waste time comparing yourself to others. Spend your energy becoming your best self. We're not all equal in talent or ability. Some of us are physically superior, others are academically superior, still others nicer looking. We're not equal in circumstance or effort or by many other measures. But acknowledging our differences does not mean that one person is more important than another. Every person is unique. Every person has eternal value.

To find your personal brand, focus on what you control—You. That's the only person you control. You are responsible for you, nobody else. We can appreciate and love our neighbors, but we are singularly responsible for ourselves. Don't get sidetracked.

Your values are expressed in your creed—what you believe. The more time you spend thinking about who you are and what you stand for, the easier it will be to sync your thoughts, words and actions. Developing your personal brand involves finding behavioral consistency.

Don't be discouraged when you fail. From time to time you're likely to fall "out of character" and say or do something that you regret. We are all flawed. We all make mistakes. We're all sinners. It happens!

Get back on the brand exercise bike and keep pedaling. Use your brand words and your creed to help you stay on track. Think about the three words or phrases that describe you. They represent your core, how you see yourself, and how you want others to see you. Memorize them so you don't even have to refer to them on paper. Who you are and what you believe are tractor beams. Stay on course.

Sometimes when we refine our brand and become more authentic, people may have negative reactions. As you modify your behavior to mesh with who you really are, some folks will not like it. Don't be deterred.

Becoming the person you were meant to be takes concentration, effort, and brutal honesty. Finding your personal truth is a test with many difficult questions. It's up to you to supply the questions, and you're the only one with correct answers.

Seeing yourself honestly requires an examination of aspects of your behavior that aren't nice to look at. We're all flawed. We all make mistakes. That's part of your brand too. You can't ignore your faults and expect that they'll go away. You know they're there, and you know which ones need attention. Start by owning your mistakes.

When I was researching my first book, I asked hundreds of people if they would share a mistake that helped them learn and grow. Less than ten percent were willing to share a mistake. They couldn't bring themselves to admit their mistakes. It's a sad commentary on the state of our culture. We all agree that we learn, grow and benefit from mistakes, and yet we refuse to acknowledge them to ourselves or in public. If you can't admit your failings, you lose the opportunity to learn from them. Failing to admit mistakes is the single biggest cause of future mistakes.

In order for others to see you the way you wish to be seen, you need to assure that your thoughts, words and actions follow your outline. It's your masterplan for your life. You make the outline. You execute the branding. You determine who you are. And that begins when you discover who you have always been.

5

Your Name Is Your Brand

My given legal name is Charles, but I've always been Charlie, named after my late uncle. My uncle Charlie died long before I was born, so I never had an emotional connection to him or his name. I never related to other nicknames—Chuck, Chucky, Chas, etc. I have always been Charlie. That's who I am.

I grew up in a very small town. When I first started working in radio as an announcer, I didn't say my name. I read news, commercial copy and liners, but there was no reason to announce my name. I was a kid. A lot of people thought my older brother was the one working at the radio station.

Besides, my last name was confusing. Because my father (Joe) didn't read or write (he spoke broken English with a French accent), he mispronounced our surname (Seraphin). He taught us to say it like "Sir-fine," which wouldn't even be a proper French pronunciation. My dad mispronounced lots of words.

Many people in town pronounced our name "Sir-fine," but I'm not sure how many of them ever saw it written. When I learned to read and write I realized that there wasn't a logical explanation for how we pronounced our family name at home. It didn't make sense, but because my dad struggled with English we never forced the issue. I introduced myself as Charlie, and most of the time that was enough.

Teachers pronounced my last name the way it's spelled. Sometimes I was kidded by my classmates who knew our family, but most people just accepted that my last name had a formal and informal pronunciation. I don't remember ever being seriously conflicted by the discrepancy. I never told people that my dad couldn't read or write. I loved him, and that was all that mattered. When I moved away, I pronounced my surname the way it's spelled.

Over the years I had some "radio names"—Charles Brown Jr., Charles Wilson, and Magic Charlie. That was the last fake name I ever used. The magic wore off, and I dumped those personas to become Charlie Seraphin. Right back where I started from.

Every day I learn more about myself. Being comfortable with myself makes it easier to focus on my purpose. I ask myself the same questions I'm recommending for you. Am I being authentic? Am I doing everything I can to be the best person I can be? Am I taking advantage of every opportunity to help others and make the world a better place?

Your name is the first sound you ever learned. Some of you might have started life thinking your name was "baby" or "goo goo," but the sound that resonates within your soul is the name you are called. When your mother cooed over you as a baby, your name was the most often repeated word in your emerging vocabulary. Just as you learned the sound of your mother's voice, her smell and touch, you learned to respond to your name. In a sense, it was your mantra. Your name is at the core of your conscious being.

Self-representation begins during the first year of life. Hearing your own name causes unusual activity in your brain. You react to your name much differently than you react to the names of other people or any other word. Your name is important. Your good name is even more important. Knowing, seeing, and hearing your name has an impact on everything you think, see and do. Your name is a psychic reflection of who you are. No other word compares.

Have you ever walked through a public place and heard someone calling your name, only to discover that they were calling someone else who shares your name? It's a weird feeling, right?

There's nothing quite as attractive to you as your name, especially when it's voiced aloud. Even people who say they don't like their name respond favorably when they hear their name. It's the most accurate verbal representation of our brand. You may use your middle name or a nickname but when we hear someone say our name, it resonates. Professional communicators and accomplished salesmen always use a person's name when they're trying to connect. Subconsciously your name captures your attention and opens you (at least initially) to the message that follows. That awareness of a specific sound is the closest thing we have to brand identity. None of the descriptive words or phrases we use to describe who we are identify us as perfectly as our name.

Spend some time considering your name. I'm not talking about the "meaning" of your name. Just consider what your name means to you. When you learn to like your name, you're more likely to have self-confidence.

Say your name quietly (aloud) to yourself. Repeat it and see if you can feel the harmony between the sound of your name and your authentic self. Your name is a basic building block. See if you can elicit different reactions simply by saying your name. Can you call yourself to attention? Does your name evoke warm and friendly feelings when you say it?

People who share your name may be like you, or they may be different. Even when you share characteristics with other people, you are totally unique. That's the beauty and magic of authenticity. Even though others have similar names, yours has been crafted and refined just for you. There may be thousands of Kawhis, Jasmines, Priscillas, and Charlies in the world, but there's only one you and only one me.

You're very different from anyone you've ever met that shares your name, and you're different from everyone who lives in your country, state, county, town, city or neighborhood—even though you may share common descriptors. You're not responsible for them, and they're not responsible for you.

Guidance counselors often caution that "you don't have to be like so and so" when they are trying to separate students from the wrong group of friends. In reality, you couldn't be like anyone else, even if you tried. You can act like other people, but as much as you may attempt to imitate behavior, nobody thinks, talks or acts exactly like you—because there has never been (and there will never be) another you.

Self-awareness is important. Connecting with yourself helps you connect to everything else. Take that drone perspective and watch yourself as you interact. Be aware of which words and gestures are authentic and befitting of your name.

Your name is your brand. If you're like most of us, it's been tarnished from time to time. Your name has been associated with some things that you're not especially proud of. You screwed up, got caught, and were embarrassed. But your name, even with a few scratches and dents, still shines. It's the original you. Say it proudly when you introduce yourself. It's the best name you have, and that's saying a lot.

6

True Friends

For most of my life, my best friends have been people that other people might describe as weird. Sometimes my best friends are popular, but more often than not, they are on the fringe of being social outcasts. They don't comply with the norms of society. Some talk a lot and some are very quiet, but they are all present in the moment when you engage them. Most of my friends are uncommonly bright, but some are not formally educated. I tend to gravitate toward smart people who are a little quirky. That's me. That's who I've always been.

I didn't always recognize that about myself. For most of my life I didn't give a second thought to the people I called friends. These days I'm a little more selective. I have made many friends over the years. My friends from childhood know me best, and my more recent friends share my core values. What do your friends have in common? What does that say about you?

People make assumptions about us based on who we associate with. It becomes especially troubling when our associates don't reflect our values. Authentic friends—the ones who count—may be very different from us, but they know who we are, share our values, and nurture our goals, dreams, and aspirations. Casual friends share our space, but not necessarily our values. In order to become your best self, it's important to have trustworthy friends who understand you and care about your wellbeing.

True friends may have known you way back when, or you may have just met. True friends know you. They support your attempt to get where you need to be. The more you can articulate your values and goals, the easier it is for them to help you choose a course consistent with your ultimate destination. If you come to the conclusion that you haven't been acting like the person you truly are, discuss it with your friends. At first, they may push back and tell you that you're doing fine. They may even like you just the way you are. But if they understand that you're seeking something deeper, they'll come around and help you toward your goal.

Bouncing ideas off a friend is a great way to sort out your thoughts. Real friends don't tell you how to think or what to do, but they remind you who you are. Real friends are the harbingers of truth and enemies of lies and lying. Like mirrors they reflect us, blemishes and all. Even if they don't always agree with you, they have a way of steering you back toward your authentic self.

If you don't have a friend you can talk to about your creed, what you truly believe, it's time to find one. Sleep on it. Search your memories. There must be someone out there that you've forgotten about. It may even be someone that you didn't think you knew that well. You'll find just the right person. It may be a surprise. You have such a friend, even if you haven't communicated in a long time. Track them down and see if you can reconstruct the relationship. If it feels awkward and difficult, it could be that you weren't as close as you remember.

There are people out there aching to have a values discussion, you just have to seek them out. Friends are always willing to listen. Two heads are better than one. You don't need judgment or direction, just honest feedback. And remember, online friends are different from true friends, and heart-to-heart discussions are different from texts, online chats, or instant messages.

One of my best friends claims that each of us has no more than five true friends. "You can count them on one hand," he used to say. They are the ones that you'd want with you walking down a dark alley in a frightening situation. True friends never desert you. They never put their own interests above your friendship. Thick and thin, they're always there for you when you need them. They always have your back.

I regularly pick up the phone and call a friend I haven't seen in years, and the experience is always pleasant. Their situation and health may change, but the core elements of our friendship remain intact. It's best to call when you aren't looking for a favor. Even if there's nothing pressing that needs sharing, reach out to someone who you knew before. You may discover a deeper friendship than you remember.

Fake friends are a different breed. We all have people we call friends, but if we're honest, we know straight away that they can't be trusted. At some point, they will betray us. We come up with reasons to justify spending time with these people. They live close. They have a car. They share mutual interests or acquaintances. They are virtual friends who regularly like our posts on Facebook or Instagram. We may have been friends over a period of time. During our "friendship" we look past their shortcomings. They serve a purpose, fill a void.

Some of them are still part of your life.

True friends usually mirror your values. Some are much more receptive to a serious discussion than others, but every true friend is interested in what you think and what you believe. That's how it goes. Some friends are just for fun. Some friends are forever. If your friend is a problem, causes you to drift from your values...separate and create space. Don't let their problem become your problem.

When you're honest with yourself, you will know which of your friends are leading you toward your goals, and which are leading you astray. Real friends push you to be your best self. Don't waste time and energy on make-believe friendships. If you find yourself saying and doing things that are completely out of character when you're with someone, maybe you shouldn't be with them.

I'm not suggesting you dump all your fake friends today but be honest. Separate true friendship from convenient relationships. It's perfectly OK if your friends have idiosyncrasies like most of my friends but distinguish between being weird and being untrustworthy. Fake friends are more dangerous than enemies.

Review the other people in your life. Don't get trapped trying to judge them. You're not reviewing their qualities as much as you are determining whether they lift you up or push you down. If you love someone who currently represents a negative influence, it may be helpful to have a heart-to-heart discussion about your goals. Explain your desire to be your best you, and make suggestions regarding how they can help you.

Your goal is to improve your progress, not to modify their behavior. If they're not receptive, don't force it. Work on you. Ask people to help you grow. Listen and reflect. Don't try to reinvent the wheel or everyone in your life.

Be patient, observant and consistent. And be aware that your efforts may not yield immediate, desirable results. It takes time to get your friends onboard with your mission to develop your personal brand. Friends can be valuable instruments of change. Use them to your benefit. And while you're at it, be a true friend to them too!

7

Brand Confusion

In 1985, in the face of shrinking market share, Coca-Cola changed its recipe and introduced New Coke. They wanted to make their product taste sweeter to better compete with rival Pepsi. It was a disaster. Because it didn't taste like Coke, and the label announced it as New Coke, the market overwhelmingly rejected the new formula and within three months Coca-Cola went back to "original formula" Coke. After getting back to their basic brand, market share soared.

Commercial product marketers often caution against "brand confusion." A consumer expects one thing from a brand, but either the advertising or the product fails to meet expectations. Appearance, color, texture, logo, format, associations, story, etc. have to remain constant in order to successfully market a brand. When large corporations venture into new areas, they often co-brand products that are inconsistent with their primary brand. That also creates brand confusion.

Consistency plays an important role in branding. Staying true to your brand is critical. If you put all your effort into external imaging, you're likely to lose sight of your authentic brand. Staying true to your original ingredients, in this case your core values, is essential.

We've all met people who demonstrate brand confusion. Who am I? What do I believe? What am I willing and unwilling to do, and why do I feel the way I do? Those types of questions probe your basic core values. It's healthy to ask. The answers reveal your authentic self. Then, just like with a commercial brand, you have to evaluate the product against a brand promise.

Achieving personal brand consistency requires that we think, talk and act consistently. If I'm a loving person, I need to think loving thoughts, speak lovingly, and act toward others in a caring and loving manner. If I think angry, hateful thoughts, it's virtually impossible to speak and act lovingly. Like any other brand, your personal brand requires much attention to detail. Coke needs to taste like Coke. Original formula "you" needs to speak and act accordingly.

In order to be the original "you," you need to behave the way you know you need to behave. Shed your disingenuous disguises. We tend to expect certain standards of behavior from other people without attention to our own brand confusion. We are regularly disappointed by others, but we seldom apply the same standards of behavior to ourselves.

In recent years we have witnessed multiple high-profile celebrities exposed as sexual predators. The scenario is repeated all too often. Outwardly these people project All-American images of family and faith, when in reality they used their power and position to force young women to submit to unwanted sexual advances. In those instances, their personal brands are forever tarnished. If I say the name, you think scumbag.

It's impossible to ascribe motives. Only the perpetrator can explain why, but it's my guess that each of those famous people started with a little lie. "It's not a big deal. Nobody will know. No harm, no foul, etc." They got away without detection and did it again. After a while, their obnoxious behavior became a habit. They justified to themselves what they did and became comfortable with their misbehavior. Even if it's not who they truly are, it's their brand from now on. We have to live with the consequences of our actions.

For most of us, our indiscretions are less serious. We all do things we regret, but our stupid mistakes are not likely to make national headlines. Big or small, it's no fun being caught in a lie. If you have committed serious transgressions, act quickly to resolve your problems. Accept responsibility and ask for forgiveness.

The little mistakes we make all contribute to our brand. The key is to eliminate the big sins and work to correct the little ones. If we're honest, there are aspects of our personal brand that we aren't proud of. While you don't need to advertise your quirks and bad habits in public, it's a serious mistake to ignore them. Simple transgressions don't make or break a brand, but little lies and bad habits have a way of tarnishing your brand over time. Think, talk, and act the way you want to be remembered. Nobody expects you to be perfect, but everyone appreciates when you are authentic.

When you take a "drone perspective" and watch yourself from the outside in and the top down, you get to know yourself. You're likely to see things that need fixing. That's what developing your personal brand is all about.

When we're honest we realize that we're not perfect. We make mistakes. We do things we wish we hadn't done. Odds are you'll mess something up down the road. We try to live a mistake-free life, but from time to time we fall off the wagon.

Avoiding mistakes takes concentration. When you aren't paying attention, unfortunate things happen. Your goals and aspirations demand a conscious effort to develop and nourish your brand. Careless mistakes and bad behavior impede your best future.

Sometimes we try to rationalize our behavior by telling ourselves that our actions didn't hurt anybody or anything. Excuses increase the odds that we'll repeat our mistakes. Avoiding future mistakes and bad behavior begins with acknowledging them in real time. Left uncorrected, our negative actions are bound to cause future pain and embarrassment. Be your best self. Pay attention.

Avoiding poor decisions is a lot easier when you think before speaking or acting. I've talked to a number of people who say they hear their mother's voice when they're faced with a decision. Some people say it's loud and clear. They hear their mother's voice warning them against doing things they know they shouldn't do.

If that sounds like you, try to move away from guilt (i.e., your mother's voice). Create a new and more consistent call to action. Work to develop your "brand voice." It will tell you if what you're doing is part of your master plan. Remember, it's not about image or what other people will think. Personal brand success isn't achieved by occasionally avoiding mistakes. Consciously direct your thoughts, words and actions. When you take charge, you are your authentic you.

You will mess up. You may do something without considering

all the possible outcomes. Those mistakes cause unintended consequences. As soon as you recognize a gap between who you are and what you're doing, take immediate corrective action. Admit your mistake. Commit to improving your behavior. Say you're sorry if you've hurt someone. Pay more attention next time.

No matter what, don't try to "re-package" or "re-formulate" yourself. The key is to be yourself. We're all flawed, and we all make mistakes (see *One Stupid Mistake* for examples), but our daily goal is to be our best self. The Coca-Cola story exemplifies what happens when you're not true to yourself or your brand. Become your best self in everything you are associated with. Don't deviate. And when you mess up, apologize, correct your error, and move on.

Strive to be "original formula you." Shoot for absolute authenticity. Sync your thoughts, words and actions with your values. That way you ensure brand consistency.

Sometimes brand enhancement is the direct result of temporary brand confusion. In other words, the recovery overshadows the initial misstep. Remember, it's not the mistake that you made in the past that makes or breaks your brand, it's your honest response and demonstrated will to make amends.

Don't forget to forgive yourself. "That was dumb," I tell myself regularly. "Why in the world did I do that?" There are as many answers as there are mistakes. Avoid the blame game and don't make excuses. Admit your flaws, commit to do better, and move on.

At the end of every day ask yourself if you accurately represented your brand. Were your thoughts harmonious with who you are? Did your words reflect your true feelings and core values?

Did you listen to your quiet little voice and act the way you know you should act? Reflect on the high point of your day. What was good about it? How did it make you feel? How can you repeat that accomplishment in the future? Then spend some time addressing the situations where you weren't your best. What happened? How can you keep it from happening in the future? Have you made amends?

You'll be amazed at how powerful a simple examination of conscience is in developing a strong, positive self-image. Protect your brand. Don't expect brand perfection. Deal with the reality of your shortcomings. Stop blaming others and making excuses. Pay attention and keep it together. Your honest, daily review of successes and failures is a healthy way to keep things in perspective.

8

Your Baby Laugh

We are born with a positive disposition. As infants, we are generally joyful. When we're hungry or hurt or we need a diaper change, we get loud, but most of the time, we find happiness in pretty much everything from the scent of our mother to flowers and clouds.

There's an urban myth that children laugh considerably more than adults, but a number of respected experts suggest that's just not true—or, at least, it doesn't have to be true.

In well-balanced homes, children are taught to laugh. Parents see the child doing something "funny" and they laugh. Before long, the child performs the act in order to get a laugh. Most times, the child laughs right along with his or her parents and everybody has a good time. No two laughs are alike.

If you grew up in a sullen home without laughter, you may have to learn to laugh. For most of us it's an unconscious reflex, but it is possible to consciously rediscover your laugh. It's one of those conscious decisions that leads to brand enhancement. We're all attracted to upbeat, positive, happy people. Nobody likes a grouch.

Some of us laugh outside social settings. For example, I laugh aloud while reading or watching TV by myself. I can appreciate humor when there's nobody around to see or agree with what strikes me as funny. Laughter isn't for other people, it's for you. Sometimes

I'm grumpy when I haven't had a good laugh. In those instances, I consciously look for things that amuse me.

It's okay to manufacture amusement with a playful spirit. You can decide to make things light-hearted and fun. While it's true that not everybody shares our sense of humor, and sometimes you need to be a little cautious and consider your audience, generally speaking we're better off laughing and having fun as often as possible.

Toddlers and very young children are less self-conscious than adults. As we age, we grow thick filters that change the way we view things. Other people influence our thinking. Objects and behaviors that we previously found funny, entertaining, and cute are judged stupid and meaningless.

It happens. Our tastes evolve. As we mature we succumb to societal pressures. That doesn't mean you have to stop laughing. You may have to find new triggers, but whatever you do, don't forget to laugh. There's plenty of sadness, tragedy and confusion in life. Laughter is a counterbalance. Everything goes better with a smile.

The past looks different through the filter of time. Your ability to retain a contemporary and honest view of yourself and the world around you is critical when you are developing your personal brand. Too often family, friends, associates, teachers, mentors, bosses, co-workers and others infuse negatives into our heads. We become sensitive and cautious and lose the ability to appreciate what's funny.

Some people become so suppressed that they can't recognize humor. When a child is repeatedly told "you're dumb" or "you're stupid," it becomes a gamble for that child to laugh out loud. Nobody wants to be ridiculed for laughing at something that might not be considered funny, so we learn to swallow our laughter reflex for fear of exposing our own ignorance.

Laughter is a tonic. Laughing is healthy. Doctors agree that laughter is not only good for our psychological health, it's good for our physiological health. Suppressing laughter is unhealthy. I don't think any of us wants to live in a world without love and laughter. Laughter is good for the body *and* the soul. This lesson is especially important for parents. Humor is multi-generational. Families that encourage laughter are healthier and happier. Pass it on.

Scientists can debate whether children laugh more than adults or whether personality type plays a larger role in whether or not we laugh. But no matter the science behind it, let's you and I make a conscious decision to laugh more often. Laughter heals even a wounded heart. Whether it is a result of social interaction or self-generated humor, it's a good idea to laugh often. It's especially good to laugh at yourself.

Laughing at yourself suggests that you've achieved a higher level of consciousness, an elevated perspective. Sometimes we say and do things that aren't right. We make mistakes. We screw up. Okay, so what? When it's a big mistake, rectify it quickly. But when it's a little oops, go ahead and laugh. Being aware of mistakes and finding humor in our humanness is a lot healthier than pretending it wasn't our fault.

Don't be pushed down by societal forces and bad experiences. If you tried something once and it didn't work, don't be afraid to try it again. If it doesn't work, regardless of how hard the task or how many different ways you tried before, give it another shot. If it still just doesn't work, have a good laugh and move on. If you are ridiculed for trying, that's not your problem.

The world doubted many of the great innovators. It takes courage to move against public opinion. When in doubt, rely on your quiet little voice to tell you whether or not to proceed. Some of the decision filters you've developed during your life are helpful, but some are harmful. It's up to you to determine the best course of action. What's right for you might not be right for other people. Having people criticize or laugh at you shouldn't matter. Following your instincts and acting in harmony with your values is most important.

Developing your personal brand demands that you stay true to who you are. That doesn't mean that you always have to be great. For example, some of us are not good dancers. And yet we all find ourselves on the dance floor once in a while. Laughing and dancing are healthy exercises, but not everybody is comfortable with either or both. It's up to you to determine who you are, and that involves things you enjoy, things you're good at, and things that you don't like.

The difference between what we love and what we fear or avoid is often the result of a negative thought planted in our head by someone else. That's why getting in touch with your values and paying attention to the authentic you is so important.

I enjoy watching other bad dancers (like me) on the dance floor. Without balance or rhythm, we're not likely to compete on one of the TV dancing shows. But even if we can't dance well, it's fun. We naturally enjoy watching people enjoying themselves. If you love to do something, go for it, and have a good time. What you enjoy is part of your personal brand, even if you're not great at it.

Every day doesn't bring sunshine and rainbows. Life does not work that way. There's likely a drop of rain for every ray of sunlight. Some experiences are enjoyable, some are not. We all have good and bad days. The key is to enjoy your positive experiences and manage your negative ones. It's an internal balance. Allow your joy to balance your sorrow, your happiness to offset the sadness that comes with living.

Sometimes we hide our feelings. We only want the world to see the happy me, and not the suffering that's part of my package. Obviously, that's counter productive. It's not about what other people see, it's what you see. Being authentic doesn't mean always putting on a happy face.

Recognize your emotions but don't confuse them with who you are. You're not angry. You feel angry. You're not depressed. You feel depressed.

Separating who you are from what you feel is one of the trickiest tasks in branding. The tools we've talked about…interpersonal communication, listening, reflection and friends can help us separate temporary feelings and emotions from the bedrock that is our brand. Some of us are more emotional than others. Some of us tend to dwell on one feeling or emotion more than others.

In your quiet moments, separate who you are from what you're feeling. Remember, you're not depressed, even when you're feeling depressed. You're not angry, even when you're feeling angry. There's a difference. When you take an "out of body" perspective and look at yourself from the outside, it's easier to distinguish feelings from who you are.

Track the number of times you laughed today and try to increase that number by one tomorrow. There are babies laughing around the world. Laugh like a baby. The more you laugh, the better you feel.

9

Your Brand Is Your Legacy

In our social media-obsessed society, we've been taught to believe that flashy images capture the big bucks. In truth, projecting an image is dwarfed by authenticity. Each day you have the choice between enhancing your image and improving your personal brand. One is fake and one is real.

You have the opportunity—and in my opinion, the obligation—to create your own authentic legacy. If you're just going through the motions, living a lie, your brand isn't based on who you are or what you believe. Your tombstone could read, "Here lies a liar, a fake and a fraud." I like to think that every person desires to be authentic. You get dozens of opportunities each day. Every time you meet someone, there's a chance to demonstrate your brand. Each situation, including your mistakes and bad decisions, creates opportunities to demonstrate character.

Whether you live to be a hundred or die young, your personal brand will be your legacy. Some people are given great ceremonies after they die. Statues are erected, events are cancelled, flags fly at half mast, and names are placed on streets and buildings. Most of us will never know such adulation, but that doesn't make your brand any less important.

There is a much higher standard than public adulation. Time

marches on. Statues are torn down and building names are changed. But your brand, thoughtfully displayed, has the potential to live forever. It will live on in the hearts and minds of every person you come in contact with. Your brand is just as important as any famous or infamous person's brand. Your brand is the only one of its kind in the history of the planet. Once and forever, you're living an experience that cannot be duplicated, altered or erased. When you step back and see the enormity of your uniqueness, it's clear that every life has meaning.

If you're confused about your brand, you're not alone. You probably know a guy who is a totally different person away from the job or a woman who says she hates doing her hair and makeup but never goes out without freshening up and putting on her face. When people don't know who they are, they confuse all sorts of imagery with being their authentic self.

Personal brands have more to do with what we do than what we say. That's why brand confusion runs rampant. It's more than being unsure how to answer the question "What do you want to be when you grow up?" It's more than the conflicting images you post on social media. You are what you think, say, and do, but your personal brand is most defined by what you do.

Sometimes we get caught up in the millions of images that bombard us every week. Social media suggests that life is glamorous. Beautiful people doing interesting things is a perceived norm. Everybody is happy and having fun. In truth, life can be difficult, and what you see and read online is often disingenuous.

We have been led to believe that the search for meaning

involves money, social standing, notoriety, and professional success. It's a lie. Climbing that mountain leads to dark and lonely cliffs. A higher percentage of rich people kill themselves than poor people. If that's where you are headed, stop, rest, think, and wake up. Being rich and famous doesn't make you happy. It is likely to make you more cautious, suspicious, and sometimes even paranoid.

Surrendering to the reality that you may never grow rich or famous isn't losing. Being fake is losing. Confusing your priorities is losing. Being unhappy because you don't have something you don't need is losing. Never reaching your potential is losing.

Winning involves connecting with your own personal values, whatever they may be, and then living every second of every day committed to demonstrating how critical those values are in your life. Developing your personal brand has little to do with how other people react to you. It's about you, being your best, finding peace and happiness in your own life. We do that by setting our own standards and achieving our own personal goals. Don't be surprised if authenticity leads to economic success. We're drawn to people who have a strong sense of who they are and where they're going.

You may decide that life is incredibly serious. Taking on the responsibilities discussed here might strike you as a difficult job. That doesn't mean you have to be humorless. You don't have to act like a funeral director. Some people think monks are always serious. Monks laugh and smile more than you might think. They love to have fun, but they are consistent in their values-driven behavior. You can be serious and fun at the same time.

If you only focus on how other people see you, it's easy to get caught up in a lie. Living for approval is a waste. Coloring up your image for other people is a lie. If you struggle with that, if your self-esteem is lacking, remind yourself daily that you're the same good person you were when you were born. Negative self-feelings or self-hate are simply layered on judgments from your past. They're cranial noise. They can be eliminated through peaceful reflection.

Here's another way to think of it. You are the sum total of all the decisions you've made up until this moment. You're the product of your environment, your experiences, your family, and your genetics. Along the way, people stuck labels on you, and tried to lay a lot of garbage on your psyche. You've already gone through the wringer of life. Some of your joy and happiness was squeezed out along the way. Too bad. It happens to the best of us. Suck it up and move on with purpose and direction. Joy and happiness can be re-infused into every life. Love yourself and others will find you lovable.

The world may give thumbs up to makeup and a well-drawn storyboard, but your reality doesn't have anything to do with image—digital or otherwise. You aren't a hologram or just another hollow mannequin. You are special and unique, one of a kind.

If the authentic you is not what others see, you have work to do. Refining your personal brand is a step-by-step, day-by-day process. You are likely to become frustrated, but whatever you do, don't give up. Make adjustments. If you have an inflated sense of self-worth, tone it down. If you are burdened with negative feelings and emotional baggage, let them go.

This chapter isn't suggesting that you shouldn't comb or color your hair or wear makeup or dress in a way that makes you more confident. There's nothing wrong with taking pride in your appearance. All I'm suggesting here is that there's more to you than what others see.

In order to reach your goal you need to devote time to observing yourself. It takes awareness and commitment. It doesn't happen online with a computer or phone. You can't find it in the digital realm. It has nothing to do with followers or likes.

You don't have to continue acting the way other people expect you to act or live out the fantasies they laid on you. Be yourself. Be honest. People will see you the way you really are when you start being completely and totally honest. You can change the way you live your brand. You can become the person you've always wanted to be.

10

Simple Tools for Brand Improvement

There are simple, easy corrective steps to get in touch with our authentic self. Here are some tools to help you, but they don't work when you're distracted. If you're driving in heavy traffic, it's not likely that you can learn an important podcast lesson. If you're about to jump out of an airplane, you may not be able to focus on important relationship lessons. You likely won't find answers to your personal problems on social media.

The best place to look is inside, and the best place to do it is outdoors. There's something about being outdoors that stimulates humans. Being outdoors helps us concentrate. The wind, clouds, sky, sun and stars are all powerful reminders that we are part of a much bigger picture.

Even if you live in the city where mechanical sounds abide, there are lots of little sanctuaries where you can hear birds and see clouds. Try finding a rooftop or a courtyard, or a park, anyplace that offers relief from the sounds of the street. Even when you can't find an ideal natural setting, try to find a safe place where you can close out the cacophony of the world. Being awake and quiet stimulates your inner you, and when you are stimulated and reflective, you're on the road to personal truth. Make it a point every day to enjoy peace and quiet.

Peace and quiet are pathways to discovering the "you" that you long to be. Mental and physical distractions abound. Combined with noises inside and outside your head, it's hard to focus. Disciplined professional athletes use focus to improve performance. When they're in the zone, the ball looks bigger, and game elements present themselves in slow motion. Until you figure out how to slow everything down, it will be difficult to get where you want to go.

Our ancestors found that solace in prayer. For thousands of years people prayed. They looked upward and toward nature to find connection with the universe and with other living creatures. In America, they went to church on Sundays and during the week they prayed while they worked in fields, shops, and factories.

You may not believe in God. You may have discarded prayer. Many people these days choose not to make time for either. But prayer and meditation have been powerful forces in this world since the beginning of recorded history. In recent times, praying in public has been ridiculed. Anti-prayer forces claim that prayer infringes on the rights of non-prayers. I often wonder if those same people would condemn Native Americans whose public prayer rituals date back more than four thousand years or Muslims whose daily prayers are heard in many urban neighborhoods.

Prayer connects more people than it divides; it always has and always will. You may choose an alternative to prayer, but if you don't find a tool that works for you, prayer is still an excellent way to connect with your quiet little voice. Most people who pray find peace.

In the 1970's, EST (Erhard Seminars Training) was a popular form of meditation. Participants reported that it helped them find themselves. There have been other more recent forms of meditation that have mirrored the effects of religious prayer. In the 1960s and 70s, it was common to see people sitting upright with crossed legs in public parks—hands on knees, fingers and thumbs touching lightly, eyes closed.

There are still those who actively meditate every day, but based on my travels, they represent a very small percentage of the population. That's a shame, because meditation has been proven to lower blood pressure and provide all sorts of psychological and physiological benefits. Many people are aware of the benefits of meditation, but they say they can't do it because it's impossible for them to "think about nothing." It's even more difficult to focus on repeating a mantra for long periods of time.

As I mentioned in Chapter Two, daily listening meditation is an easy habit to develop and a sure way to break the spell of the cacophony of the digital age. Listening to one distant sound creates harmony and focus in our brain. If you've never just sat, closed your eyes, and listened, give it a try. For a lot of people, listening is a form of prayer.

Several close friends have told me that they'd never prayed and didn't know where to begin. I told them that praying is simply talking with God. It doesn't have to be in a church or with other people. There are no essential words. In its purest form, prayer is a private conversation.

One friend asked me to teach him to pray on his deathbed. He tried, but his pain was so severe that he couldn't concentrate. That made him frustrated. Another person I spoke with recently said that when he was diagnosed with stage four throat cancer, he started praying constantly. He told me that if God didn't know his name before that, he certainly knew it by the time the doctors declared him cancer free.

Another person was facing an extreme family crisis. It looked as if there was no hope, and she was completely distraught. She said she had been praying. Whether there was any cause and effect, or whether it was just one of those things, within a couple days of our conversation, she called to report that something totally incredible and unexpected had happened. What seemed like an unsolvable problem had been favorably resolved.

Don't wait for an emergency to create a plan for dealing with a crisis. Waiting until you're on your deathbed is a serious mistake. Whether it's a conversation with God, meditation, listening or remembering, use your tools. Practice makes perfect.

If you haven't prayed before, here's a simple format. "Hey, God. You and I have never met, but I'm here…and obviously you're there. I have some things weighing on my heart and mind. I hope you know what I'm talking about. I'd like to find some peace so I can be a better person, but I might not be able to do it without your help."

If you learn how to pray or meditate regularly without the pressure of an emergency, you'll have an outlet when you encounter life's rough waters. I can't guarantee results in every situation. Not all prayers are answered the way we'd like them to be answered. I'm certain, however, that using the tools outlined here won't hurt. Learn how to use them. Each tool has the potential to bring comfort in life's most stressful situations.

If prayer, meditation, and listening don't work for you, there's an exercise I call "remembering." Remember yesterday. Remember last week. Remember last month, last year, five years ago, ten years ago, and let your mind remember the "you" that used to live in your body. Whatever the image, whatever the event, whatever the situation, when you go back and then back even further, you'll come to special memories. How were you acting? What were you thinking back then? Can you get in touch with the "you" that was before? Here's an example:

I remember standing at the end of a dock that jutted out into the backwaters of the Wisconsin River. It was like a lake, but there was a constant current in the middle as the river flowed south. The dock was fairly long, so standing there, I had the feeling of being disconnected from the shore. As the currents moved the water beneath me, the wind would lift the edges of nearby lily pads. Standing alone, on the end of the dock, I would bow to each of the four directions. It was a ritual that seemed natural to me as a child. I'm not sure where I got the idea, but there was something about being out on the water with wind and sky that moved me to feel respect and gratitude.

North, south, east and west are logical divisions of the natural universe. They represent powerful forces beyond the limitations of human understanding. As the water moved below my feet, I felt connected to every natural element. My memories of those experiences are clear, but I can't for the life of me understand where bowing to four winds came from. There are many forces in nature that are beyond understanding. Respect for higher powers is basic to the human condition. It's completely normal to have feelings without rational and logical explanations. That's part of what makes you... well, you.

When you think back, where do your memories take you? Can you find a spot on your life's timeline where you were in harmony with your surroundings? Can you remember your safe place or a time of extreme joy?

It won't happen in one session. There's no timetable for remembering, but the more often you can find that quiet space, listen, and then remember, the more likely you are to begin to connect with your authentic self. In the past, you may have conjured up memories in order to be critical of other people. Keep others out of your remembering exercises. You are only looking to connect with yourself at a previous time. Focus on you, nobody else.

Try to remember one primary feeling. When you find it, remember it. The more often you can experience your primal feeling, the more successful your endeavor to become your original, authentic you. If you have a hard time remembering, you can pray about it. "Dear God, help me remember. I'll be quiet now and wait for your answer."

Identifying your spiritual brand is critical. It doesn't have to have a name and you don't have to belong to any group. Your spiritual brand encompasses every value that you hold dear. It's all your aspirations. Your spiritual brand involves fundamental feelings based on core beliefs. Seek them through peace, quiet, listening, remembering, prayer or meditation. Connect to your roots. Relax and observe. Daily routine. Practice makes perfect.

11

Hitting Bottom

Some lucky people bounce off the bottom. Sometimes during an event, or simply by the grace of God, they awake to acknowledge serious problems and take corrective action. Other people carry their addictions to their graves.

Before I was born, my father was a binge drinker who would go days without sleeping when he was on a bender. He had a serious problem. As the story goes, my mom gave him the "This Way or the Highway" speech, and he quit drinking. Cold turkey, on the spot, he never took another drink in his life. I never knew him as an alcoholic. He was a great dad, not perfect by any means, but he was smart and fun and loving. If he could do it, you can do it.

There is no limit to the capacity of a person who believes she can. Attitude is everything. If my dad, a confirmed alcoholic, could quit drinking cold turkey and forever, then you can shed your worst habits too. Your personal brand is at your command, but your transformation may not be instantaneous. You may have to work for days, weeks or months to modify your behavior. You may struggle. Listening exercises, prayer, meditation, and remembering are helpful tools. You can succeed. Guaranteed.

If you put in the time and effort, there's no reason you can't find the constant "I" that has been you from the beginning of time.

I wish I could imagine all the challenges that you face. I wish I could reach out and heal your wounds and take away your pain. But that's not real. Sometimes it's easier to deal with physical pain. You can isolate it. You can bandage it, or a physician can diagnose and treat it. Emotional pain is more difficult. You can't see it. Often you don't know where it came from. It's just a dull, aching feeling. It permeates every cell. It's awful.

So now what? Like everything else, it's up to you. Will you feed it and encourage it and watch it grow to consume you, or will you get back in that drone and find a higher perspective? The more you concentrate on emotional pain, the stronger it grows. In order to move past it, you're going to have to put it out there in front of you. Examine it without emotion. What's going on? What can I control? What aspects of the problem are beyond my control.

We can control and rise above what ails us. If you give it your full attention, you can figure things out and move on. If you are fortunate you have a friend who will help you organize your thoughts and work through your problems.

Unfortunately, some friends aren't much help. They mean well, but then they ask you to relive a traumatic experience and then tell you how sorry they are. That doesn't help. Sometimes friends offer specific advice, but there's a fifty-fifty chance they'll send you in the wrong direction.

If you can't figure it out on your own or with a friend, find a professional counselor you trust. Choose carefully.

If it's any consolation, I don't think I've ever known a person who hasn't bounced off the bottom at some point in life. Dark clouds form in clear skies. Bad things happen to good people. Happiness can be shattered by unexpected sadness. It's all part of the cycle of life. But before you allow yourself to become melancholy or depressed, remember this very important truth: You are the master of your mind. Your brain is an organ. You are the organ master. It can't play any tune without you. It can't think any thoughts without your permission.

One of the benefits of building a strong personal brand is that you can take pride in your work. When you connect with your values and live your life accordingly, you build up immunity against the negatives that come into every person's life. From time to time we all get sick. If we are healthy and our antibodies are functioning at full force, we recover.

It's time to get healthy. It's time to take stock of your flaws, weaknesses and bad habits and flush your system. The cleaner your mind and heart, the better your chances of surviving the next storm. We all feel pain, even when we don't deserve it and are not prepared. It happens. At the monastery we fasted regularly. A liquid-only diet for twenty-four hours is a simple way to clear a lot of toxins from your body. Sometimes it takes a day dedicated to meditation and prayer to flush your brain.

I don't know what's happened to you in the past or what might happen in the future, but I know that if you sync your values with your actions your chances of survival increase exponentially. If you get your emotional house in order now, you'll be prepared. If you have old emotional baggage, take it out, look it over, then dump it.

Don't look back, it's not worth your time or energy. Keep your eye on the prize. The future is yours to shape. Shape it wisely.

12

Your True Self

"Fake it 'til you make it" is a popular mantra for our current era, but it's a lie. It's easy to spot people who are trying to be something they're not.

Often when we record people's voices for the first time, they hear themselves and say, "That's not me. I don't sound like that!" Or when they see photos of themselves they ask, "Oh God, do I look like that?" In their minds they have a different self-image. You can choose to pay attention, or you can continue to pretend.

It's healthy to see yourself the way you are—your strengths and your weaknesses. As strange as it sounds, it may take time to get used to that person. We have an image of ourselves that may or may not be accurate. You may have come to believe that you're the person others want you to be, but inside you're really not that person at all.

My suggestions are intended to open your mind to the possibility that whether you are young or old, whether you have your act together or if you're kind of a mess, you can become more authentic. You're one of a kind, a very special and unique person. Warts and all, you're beautiful, worth getting to know, and capable of being better than you have ever been.

Some of us have thicker skin than others, but at some level, everybody likes to be acknowledged, loved and appreciated. We care about how we are perceived. We are instinctively aware of the way people react to us. Instincts are triggered by everything from facial expressions and body language to words. Those instincts produce chemical reactions in our brain.

People who say they don't care what others think about them are lying. We like to think we've evolved, and some of us are better at hiding our feelings, but deep down we all react to what other people say and do, especially when they say things about us and do things to us. We can learn not to show feelings, but we have them nonetheless. The question is: how do we react?

Sometimes our reactions take us out of authentic mode. We pretend. In *One Stupid Mistake*, I made the point that even smart people do dumb things. One of the most frequent dumb things people do is pretend to be somebody they're not. Regardless of how good you are at pretending you're probably not fooling anybody. Just as we instinctively know when people like or dislike us, we instinctively spot phonies. Even if you can't put your finger on it, you know.

The same instincts that cause us to react to phony people draw us to authentic people. We are instinctively attracted to genuine people who are consistently themselves. They're the same people every time we interact with them. That just feels good.

Authentic people are surrounded by love. They are upbeat. When we are around them, we feel better. Real people understand who they are. Their personal vibe sets everyone else at ease.

Authenticity is attractive to humans, fakery is not. If it isn't authentic, it's fake. As you strive to develop your brand, it's vital that you are honest with yourself about what you are and what you are not. Truth is critical to the process.

I managed a radio station in Hollywood. Many people I met and worked with were always "in character." They were friendly and polite, but it was obvious that they weren't going to let you behind their protective barriers. I hired a DJ named the Real Don Steele. He always dressed in black. He called everybody "baby." He was incredible on the air—funny, bright, and always on cue—but he was never "off." In the years I worked with him, I never saw him out of character. He was a good guy and a great DJ, but if you asked me about him, I'd have a hard time explaining anything more about him than what I heard on the radio. I loved his work, but I honestly didn't know him. I liked him a lot, but I was never able to probe his personal brand.

There were a few notable exceptions, but for the most part the other Hollywood celebrities I met were always on. That doesn't mean they are bad people, just professionals, doing their thing. Entertainers can't afford to have bad days. They have an image. It's their job to live up to expectations every time they are in public. They protect their brand image, but that doesn't always equate to who they are in private. It's probably the same with people you know. Some appear to be acting. For others, what you see is what you get.

Some of the most successful Hollywood stars are authentic. They've developed personalities that reflect who they are, so they don't have to pretend. When they act, they act naturally. They can portray different characters, but there's always an underpinning of their own personality in each role. They've learned that being yourself is easier than pretending to be someone you're not.

When you meet them, it's like meeting an old friend, somebody you already know. They're funny and interesting and easy to talk with. There were a number of celebrities who fit that mold. I remember a chat with Bruce Willis about raising children. He was sitting with his wife and newborn baby at a restaurant. We were sitting close, our chairs almost touching. As the father of six, I couldn't help but admire the way he held his daughter. When he saw me smiling at the baby, he passed the baby to his wife and struck up a conversation. I always pictured him as a down to earth, friendly guy. He didn't disappoint. He was sincerely interested in our conversation. He was proud and excited about being a dad. Without an ounce of pretense, he shared his excitement with a stranger.

When you watch TV and movies, see if you can determine which of your favorite actors is most comfortable in a role. Chances are if you met them offstage, they'd be the same person you saw on the screen. Live your values. Express your beliefs. Be yourself.

13

Everyday People

"I missed the bus" can be either a negative or a positive experience, depending on your attitude. I like to think that I'm exactly where I'm meant to be doing exactly what I'm supposed to be doing. It's not good or bad, but the results are always interesting. It wasn't always that way. I've had airplane cabin doors close in my face. I've waved at the train as it was leaving the station without me. It used to upset me. Actually, it used to piss me off to no end. I'm not sure when, but somewhere along the way I learned to relax. Life is a lot easier when you're not fighting with reality.

Sometimes things work out the way we plan, and sometimes not. When we stop worrying about what other people are thinking and concentrate on our own actions, we realize that the only thing we control is how we react to unexpected reality. When that plane door closed in my face, I sat and stared at it for what seemed like hours. I was angry and thought my will power could convince someone to reconnect to the gate and let me board. It wasn't until the plane lifted into the air headed toward my destination without me that I came to grips with my reality. All the time I spent fretting was wasted and gone, and the disappointment took a bigger toll than the few hours I had to spend at JFK waiting for the next flight.

Controlling emotions comes with practice. When life presents a hurdle, I still feel that split second of agitation, but I'm more apt to see the situation for what it is. That's not to say I've reached nirvana, but my brand behavior is much better than it has ever been—and not as good as it will be tomorrow. That's the fun in personal brand development. It's like a jigsaw puzzle that constantly calls for another piece. As you patch up and fix up different aspects of your character, you find new areas that need attention. I like the jigsaw puzzle analogy better than whack-a-mole. It's the difference between frustration and the satisfaction of steady improvement. Let's enjoy getting better at being who we are.

I normally greet people, even if they are strangers, as I pass them. Some respond, but some just keep walking. Their response doesn't have value or meaning one way or the other. I choose to say hello, but after that it's just observation. If they say hello and they are conversant, great. If they look the other way and keep walking, great. It's all part of that moment, that day. I respect your right to act the way you act. I won't judge you because you think, talk or act differently than I do. I might think about it and even wonder aloud, but I've come to understand that I am only responsible for myself and my behavior. When I'm my best self, people in my world tend to react positively.

We all know individuals who fret and analyze for hours, days, and even weeks if they say hello and are ignored. Some react in anger. Some react with tears. Many people spend inordinate time trying to "understand" what was going on in the mind of another person. That's a waste of energy. You can never truly understand other people's thoughts and actions. They might have been daydreaming and missed your greeting. Maybe they didn't hear you. Give them the benefit of the doubt. Why waste energy creating a false narrative that has nothing to do with the reality of the situation? It's not a big deal. It happens all the time. Let it go.

That's why it's so important to focus first and foremost on your personal brand. It takes time and practice to concentrate on yourself in a constructive, critical manner. It takes time and patience to learn to understand yourself. When you learn to control your thoughts, your words and actions follow naturally. Before you know it, you'll be living the life you've chosen. When you spend time trying to analyze, critique and understand why other people are doing what they do, you're taking your eyes off the prize.

That doesn't mean there won't be bad days full of incredible challenges. You just can't predict what life will toss your way. One minute you're riding high, and the next minute you're flat on your back. The person who amazed you yesterday may disappoint you today.

When you're in a rut and pressure is building inside your head, don't lose hope. Before you go too far down your rabbit hole, take a minute to review. Get in that drone perspective and rise out of yourself. Look down from a higher point of view. If you feel like the weight of the world is on your shoulders, take a deep breath. Use one of your tools (prayer, listening, meditation, remembering) to break the negative cycle. Take a walk outside or go out at night and look at the stars. Get away from noise and light pollution and see a clear night sky. Nature helps us find perspective.

When you have stabilized after one of life's knockdown punches, your first attention should be your thoughts. What are you thinking these days? Besides self-pity and mild depression, what else are you thinking about? Shift your thoughts from hopelessness and despair, anger or frustration, away from what might happen in the future, and concentrate for a few minutes on right now—this very minute.

You get to choose. Start with your senses. What do you see, hear, smell, taste, touch, etc. Zero in on something. Don't attach any feelings or judgments; just stay with the reality of whatever it is you see or hear or smell or feel. Observe it, examine, explore, absorb. Remember: nobody can read your mind or control what you think. Your mind is a completely private space. You are the sole master of your thoughts. You are in control of and completely responsible for what you think.

In a wonderful essay titled "An Attitude of Gratitude Brings Opportunities," Dr. Wayne Dyer suggests that if you change the way you look at things, the things you look at change. Dr. Dyer is one of the great thinkers of our generation, and this notion is one of the most important on the road to being authentic. Negative thoughts are fertilizer for bad days. Like weeds in a garden, left unchecked, they tend to take over. Dr. Dyer tells us to say "thank you" when we first awake every morning.

What are you saying "thank you" for? Everything! Life! Another day above ground. A fresh start. A chance to improve on yesterday. Anything and everything!

When you are awake and aware, there's so much to be grateful for. I've read stories about saints who thanked God when they experienced pain. That might sound pretty crazy... until you try it.

When I bump my head or cut my finger, for years my first reaction was to utter an expletive. Then, after reading Dr. Dyer's essay, I tried saying "thank you." Believe it or not, an attitude of gratitude actually makes it hurt less! Why? Because saying thank you reminds us that we're not dead. The pain didn't knock us out. It didn't leave us critically injured. It could have been so much worse. We were fortunate. We were lucky. We're still here. Whatever caused the pain wasn't the end of the road. And for that, we give thanks. Try it!

As Dr. Dyer points out, an attitude of gratitude attracts others who also demonstrate positive energy. Our mind actually generates frequencies that look for and attract new opportunities. Your personal brand is reinforced by positive energy. Your attitude, from morning 'til night, is the most important component of becoming your best you. When your attitude is gratitude, you'll be healthier, happier, and destined for all kinds of wonderful adventures and little miracles.

I once worked with a woman who was in charge of operations at a major sports facility. Everyone and everything that came into the stadium was funneled through her department. She dealt with a large staff of part-time employees, and all the vendors servicing the stadium and delivering products. The look on her face was always the same. She looked angry. When you met her for the first time you knew that she lived in a constant state of "pissed off."

After I worked with her for a couple years, I learned that it was part of a defense mechanism that she developed to protect herself. She was really a nice person (deep down under her disguise), but she created a safe zone around herself by taking on a harsh persona with a scowling facial expression. It worked for her. Nobody tried to get away with anything, and she ruled her empire without incident. Unfortunately for her, in addition to keeping employees, vendors and deliverymen in line, she also alienated nearly everyone she came in contact with. Nobody likes to be around angry, grumpy people.

It's important to say "thank you" to those around you and say it often. And when you say it, say it with a smile. Smiling is an expression of pleasure, happiness, joy, sociability or amusement. It's a way to attract other like-minded people. As I learned watching professional announcers over the years, a physical smile will change the shape of your words so that people who hear you can actually hear that smile. If you have a recording device, try it. Record a sentence without a smile, then record the same sentence with a big ear to ear smile on your face. You'll clearly hear the difference.

When you smile, the whole world smiles with you. Smiles are disarming. We are naturally attracted to people who smile. Smiling accomplishes more than charming strangers. A smile on your face demonstrates an attitude of gratitude. A smile is a sign of peace.

Start in the morning and smile throughout the day. Remember, it only takes seventeen facial muscles to smile. It takes forty-three to frown. Smiling also releases endorphins, serotonin and natural pain killers. These neurotransmitters make us feel good. Physically—for real. Smiling elevates your mood, relaxes your body and reduces physical pain. Smiling is guaranteed to improve your day, including your physical performance.

Most of us don't smile nearly enough. We have frown lines and wrinkles from scowling. If you want your personal brand to shine, smile.

14

Understanding Your Dreams

Dreams say a lot about who we are. They tell us things that are often hidden from our conscious self. On your journey to discover your personal brand, I strongly recommend that you learn to recall and catalog your dreams. We dream for a reason, and we need to pay attention.

For centuries, wise people have wondered why we dream, and what dreams mean. While we don't have clear cut answers, most everyone agrees that dreams provide a key to who we are. When we dream, the management portion of our brain is still. That's why we are often moved by other forces in our dreams and unable to physically act. You may be flying through the air toward a mountain, but you're unable to change your trajectory. Skeptics say dreams are just noise—neural activity as our brain conducts downtime diagnostics. Sometimes that may be true, but there's growing evidence that people who work to recall and catalog the frequency and content of their dreams enjoy significant benefits.

Historians point out that dream recall and sharing played a critical role in pre-industrial cultures. Fire-making and many other ancient discoveries have been directly linked to dream recall. Psychologists tell us that we can extract meaning and use our dreams to help build stronger social connections. Healthy dreamers wake up inspired and energized. Because dreams are often abstract and non-linear, they require more effort to understand than most of the things we experience when we're awake—although there are many puzzling occurrences in our waking world as well!

Healthy dreams, dream recall, recording, and dream sharing are part of healthy living. If you're hoping to discover 'the essence of you,' dreams are another tool.

The more you are in tune with your external environment, the more likely you are to remember your dreams. Pay attention. Wake up. Listen. Watch and see. The higher your level of consciousness during the day, the better your chances of remembering your dreams. The desire to understand yourself (and others) is enhanced when you remember your dreams. If you want to recall dreams, you have to consciously think about remembering them. The more you desire to remember, the more you will remember.

Over the years I've observed thousands of people who go through life as if they are sleepwalking. They move from place to place, staring straight ahead, eyes wide open, without seeing anything. When they arrive, you can ask them what they saw on the way, and they can't recall.

"How was your day?"
"OK."
"What did you do?"
"Oh, nothing really."
"What did you experience?"

"Nothing."
"Can you remember anything special?"
"Not really."

And so it goes. Another day of waking, doing, eating and sleeping without really experiencing anything.

Now imagine a day that starts with a vivid recollection of an incredible dream. You don't have to interpret it or even try to make sense of it, but simply remembering your dream sets the tone for the day. Now you're awake. Now you can pay attention to everything you see, hear, smell, touch, taste and consider. Your world comes alive, and you are the central character. Instead of the dream world acting on you, you control your conscious world. It's a subtle but powerful distinction.

Dreams and dream content are often the embodiment of a person's whole personality. When we pay attention to dreams, we find reflections of what's going on in our waking life. If I had to guess, I'd say your dream-self may be closer to your personal brand than your waking-self. Your dreams are more uninhibited. They showcase unbridled concerns and emotions and often get right to the crux of the matter. Dreams tell us things about ourselves that may be hidden from our conscious self.

Just as dreams predict future illness, promote creativity, solve problems, give us insight and help us work through stress, dreams can help discover true feelings and dispositions. Dreams provide an important tool in our quest for self-knowledge and understanding. Pay attention to your dreams. Write them down and share them. Use them as a tool in the process of finding the authentic you.

Before you go to sleep tonight, remind yourself that you want to remember your dream when you awake. Say it to yourself. "When I wake up, I am going to remember my dream."

If you hold that thought as you drift off to dreamland, your odds of remembering your dream are much enhanced. Try it. It's a great way to get a fresh start every morning as you create a stronger connection with your authentic self.

15

Think Thoughts Through

I once heard a wise man suggest that you are the sum total of your choices up until this point in your life and that your future is the sum total of choices that you make from this point forward. That applies equally to your personal brand. Just because you've been negative or done embarrassing things doesn't mean you can't turn it around. Each day presents new opportunities.

Before you share your everyday thoughts with someone else, share them with yourself. Be conscious of your thoughts to the point of directing them: "I'm going to think about (fill in the blank) and nothing else. My thoughts are not good or bad, they are just thoughts, and they belong to me." Once you learn to control your thoughts, you will experience a sense of relief.

You have the choice between negative and positive thoughts, between love and hate, joy and anger. Regardless of how much time you spend around other people or in group settings, most of the time it's just you and your thoughts, alone, uninterrupted, and unmonitored. If you can't eliminate negative thoughts and self-doubt today, resolve to work on it tomorrow.

With that perspective, let's try to lay out a plan. What would you like to think about? What subject is interesting to you? How will you direct your thinking? You get to choose. The mere fact that you are in control of your thoughts may bring a feeling of gratitude. You get to think about what you want, and not something that someone else is pushing on you. Scientists tell us that we make thirty-five thousand decisions each day. Each conscious decision is a chance to build a remarkable brand.

Here's a simple outline: The past is gone, there's nothing you can do to change it. The future is an illusion. It isn't real, and no matter how much you try to guess what might happen, there is no way to accurately predict the future. That leaves us with the present—this very moment, right now. Now you tell me what's worth thinking about.

At this moment, you are reading words on a page that I wrote. I may never know you, but now we are inexorably connected through time and space. My past is connected to your present. You are reading my thoughts. But even though we're connected, your decisions regarding what you think, say and do are independent of my decisions. What you've read will hopefully move you closer to being authentic, but that's always up to you. You're in control and you are responsible. I'm making suggestions, but your choices are the only ones that count. All the power resides in you. My suggestions can't do anything. What you do with them is all that counts.

Think healthy thoughts. I can't tell you what healthy thoughts are for you; only you can determine that. But if a thought makes you fearful, angry, resentful, or anxious, it's obviously not healthy. Here are some thoughts I enjoy spending time with: peace, quiet, fragrance, beautiful colors, favorite people, clouds, the beach and calm. Anything having to do with those thoughts tends to make me relax. Our brains are amazing. We have the ability to direct our thoughts, but more often than not we're like a truck heading downhill without brakes. We go from one negative thought to the next, and before you know it we've imagined all sorts of horrible results.

Spend some quiet time every day just thinking peaceful, relaxing thoughts. There's enough real stress in the world without manufacturing more in your imagination. When you find yourself drifting into negative "what if" scenarios, focus on the reality of the moment and replace the negative with a positive. Feel good. Feel connected. Be grateful.

There are many references in the Bible to chasing out demons. One of my favorites is from Matthew. Loosely translated, it says if you chase out a demon and leave the house clean and empty, the original demon will return and bring along seven of his demon friends. The story is illustrative of what happens with negative thoughts. If you just try to chase out the negative thought, before you know it you'll have seven more to go along with it. The key is not only to dump the negative but to replace it with one or more positives. When you worry about what might happen, you get absorbed in a series of negative scenarios.

As soon as you find yourself projecting negatives into your future, stop and take control. Physically putting a smile on your face helps. Smiling triggers mechanisms in your brain. With practice, you can quickly break free of negative thoughts. After you've put on a happy face, happy thoughts will help you keep it there.

Taking control of your thoughts is critical, especially when you are working on your personal brand. Negative thoughts stunt your brand development. Negative thoughts are often debilitating. If you want to be in a position to successfully manage negative and hurtful things that other people say to you, you need first to eliminate negative self-talk. When you find yourself fearful or doubting, that's the time to put your foot down. Out with fear and doubt, in with a positive. Take control. It's your brain, your thoughts, and you are the boss. Once you've managed your own thoughts, you're better prepared to take control of negative social situations. You can use the same techniques in both scenarios. You can even say the same words. "No, I'm not focusing on that. I prefer to think about this instead."

As you learn to become the master of your mind, you will find all sorts of simple mind games that help you deal with stress. It's OK to occasionally let your mind just wander. Just remember to keep it away from negatives. Successful people in every walk of life have given testimonials about the power of positive thinking. It's not hocus pocus. It really works. All it takes is a little desire and a conscious effort to control your mind.

Awareness combined with your desire to improve is guaranteed to yield incredible results. You didn't come into this world thinking poorly of yourself. That's somebody else's garbage. It's your life, your brand, and your choice. You have the power, but nothing happens until you make it happen.

16

Be Present

Fr. Tom Willis, a Catholic priest in St. Augustine, Florida, shared a lesson with me that he learned while attending the seminary before being ordained. One of his mentors encouraged him to say "present" every morning, as he slid his legs over the side of the bed and prepared to stand. It was a prayerful reminder that the day was underway, and he should be conscious of where he was, what he was doing, and how it would impact others.

Being present means being aware. Have you ever realized in mid-morning that you were sleepwalking through the first half of the day? Did you ever pull into the parking lot at work and become aware that you didn't see or notice anything along the way? Have you daydreamed through a telephone conversation and forgotten what was said? Unless we make a conscious effort to be present, we're likely to fall into a routine. If that routine includes unhealthy thoughts and behavior, then we're off to the races even before we have the opportunity to chart our course. We get sloppy and lazy. Being mentally lazy is the most common way to destroy your personal brand.

Wake up and stay present. Start by remembering your dream. In the few minutes after you awake in the morning and before you

move to get out of bed, recall your dream. Then, remind yourself to be present just as your feet first touch the floor.

Whatever your routine, build in some consciousness markers. If you head to the bathroom, pay attention to your physical environment and what you're doing. Splash some water on your face and look in the mirror. There you are. That's what you have to work with today. See if you notice any changes from the time you went to bed. Look at, and more importantly, observe yourself. Getting dressed, eating breakfast, morning exercise and your entire routine can become a series of conscious activities. By the time you start the business of your day you are already actively conscious of directing your brain. It's not running the show, you're in charge.

Stay present in the moment. When your mind drifts, pay attention to where it's going and then reign it in. Consciously direct your thoughts. We all think about and plan our day, look at the clock, and count down to the first obligation or scheduled activity. That's OK, but don't allow yourself to get lost in future thoughts. Stay in the moment. Look at the door as you open it. Survey the landscape when you step outside. Look around when you're inside. Use all your senses to absorb your environment and the world around you. The more aware you are of your environment, the more you're in control of your actions. You can choose the right course of action simply by being aware of all the options.

The simple act of being present and staying present will not only change your attitude; it will change the way others react to you. Keeping a journal is another way to consciously control your thoughts, words and actions. As you record them, negative and positive patterns will emerge. The simple act of writing things down helps keep you in the present. You're the only one who can keep your thoughts in check.

If you let yourself get too far ahead, you miss what's right in front of you. Once awareness becomes a habit, you won't have to ask, "Did I forget my purse or wallet, glasses or phone?" or "Did I lock the door or close the garage?" Those forgetful mornings are a sure sign that you were so busy planning what hasn't happened yet that you ignored what was happening in real time. Feet on the floor, mind on the task at hand, focus on you—your thoughts, words, and actions, and awareness of everything around you.

Most of us use a mirror more than once a day. Normally it's just a glance to see if there's food stuck in our teeth or if our hair is messed. Sometimes we use a full-length mirror to see whether our outfit works or if a top goes with the bottom we're wearing. I'm suggesting a more conscious activity.

The next time you look in the mirror, take a close look at your own eyes. Try to see yourself the way that other people do. Is the person you're looking at the person you always wanted to be? What is the difference between the person you see and your ideal you? Sometimes we need to look deep to see our best self. Sometimes it takes years.

One step at a time, one minute at a time, one day at a time.

17

Look Into My Eyes

I met a man the other day. Within fifteen seconds I knew that I would like him. I knew that he was kind, thoughtful, honest and had the potential to become a great friend. And all that came from looking at his eyes. Do you look people in the eye?

Too often, we find ourselves staring at the screen of our phone. When you're absorbed in your phone, you miss a lot. At least on a video call you can look at the other person and see if they're looking at you. When we communicate through text, we're reading words. Typing words falls far short of having a conversation. I know it's fast and easy, but there are an infinite number of things that can go wrong. You lose context. You have to interpret meaning. Worst of all, you can never be confident that your message was accurately conveyed. How many times do people say, "I talked to…" when what they mean is that text messages were exchanged? Texting, in itself, is not bad, but it should not be your primary method of communication. Honest, transparent, truth-oriented communication is best conducted face to face.

Looking into someone's eyes, reading their body language, hearing the tone and subtle qualities of their voice is a huge part of human communication. If you close a window and draw the shade, it's impossible for someone on the outside to see what's happening inside. In the same manner, it's impossible to accurately read a person's intentions when you can't hear their voice or see them.

Maybe face-to-face makes you uncomfortable. Maybe it's easier for you to look down when you pass a stranger on the street. Remember that looking into someone's eyes is the fastest way to know their intentions. When your personal brand is visible, it's easy for others to know you.

As you begin to practice "eye observation" you'll learn that each person's eyes are totally unique. You'll see them in the context of their face, but you'll also see eyes as the windows to the soul that they are. Looking into a person's eyes enhances interaction. People who are comfortable with eye contact are comfortable with who they are. When two people engage in conversation that includes their eyes, it's likely to be deeper. Even a casual glance at one another is better than looking away.

Some people may make you feel uncomfortable, and you may occasionally make others uncomfortable. That's OK. Subconscious communication is important too. When you "read" a person's eyes, you know instantly if there's a connect or disconnect.

Try to make eye contact. If it feels awkward, move on. I'm not talking about flirting with your eyes, just being respectful and interested. Eye contact stimulates transparency. You and I can look at one another and communicate without using words. Every once in a while, we look into another's eyes and feel connected. And when two people really connect, life gets interesting. Authentic people connect with other authentic people. When you look through an open window, you might see things you have never seen before. Sometimes you'll see sadness or concern, sometimes joy or fear. There are as many variances as there are people in the world.

Trust is established through eye contact. Some romantic connections begin with eye contact. Whatever your experience, it's bound to be more impactful than looking the other way. Even though you're working on your personal brand, eye contact reminds us of our connectedness. Connections are important. They transcend time and space. There are people you see only once and never forget. There are others you meet who exude a feeling that you have known them forever. Every encounter is an opportunity. The more you look, the more you see. The more you see, the better your chances of making lifelong friends.

Try to make a conscious effort to establish eye contact with at least one new person every day. It may sound simple, but this is a lot tougher than you might think. If you can do it, you are on the road to a major breakthrough. You don't have to stare, and you don't have to make a big production out of it, but you'll quickly find yourself noticing things about people that you would surely have missed if you hadn't looked directly into their eyes.

When you pay attention to a person's eyes, you see the world and the people in it in a unique way. When they look at you, their eyes shed light on who you are. Your personal brand is reflected in the eyes of other people. There's no doubt, the eyes have it!

18

Mother Teresa

Mother Teresa visited San Francisco in 1987. I was the news director at KCBS, and we broadcast her speech live from St. Mary Cathedral. By that time, she was old and frail. It was hard to imagine that such a small figure could have such a big impact on the world. She was kind and unassuming. She spoke in a whisper, but everyone in that huge church heard her every word. What's even more remarkable is her personal story.

Agnes was a tiny girl with a big dream. Her father died when she was eight. She dreamed of traveling far away. When she was eighteen she traveled to Ireland to learn English. She then traveled to India to learn more languages. She became a teacher and spent her twenties and thirties teaching young children. She became a nun and took on a new name, Sister Teresa. She became a school principal. Throughout her life, Agnes longed for something more. She was driven, but unclear about her purpose. She knew that she was destined to do something important, but it took many years for her to discover her calling. She constantly sought to discover her authentic self, to fulfill her life's mission. She prayed every day for answers.

One day, while traveling on a train, she looked out the window and saw hundreds of poor people living in squalor. They were dirty, starving, and riddled with disease. At that moment, nearly forty years into her life journey, her mission was clear. Agnes found her purpose. In a sense, she discovered her personal brand. With no management training or resources, she set out to found an organization that would change the world. She won a Nobel Peace Prize, recruited thousands of devoted followers, and touched the lives of millions of people on every continent.

Today the Catholic Church remembers her as Saint Teresa, but for those of us fortunate enough to have lived in her world, she will always be Mother Teresa—a tiny, frail, woman with a wrinkled face, a magnetic personality, and a powerful message.

Each of us has a calling. There's a quiet little voice inside that regularly reminds us that our time and place on earth is not accidental. Too often we suppress those feelings. We ignore the quiet little voice as it nags at us from deep inside. Cynics will tell us that it doesn't matter. They'll try to convince you that there's no rhyme or reason, purpose or destiny. They'll tell you to live for today and collect as much as you can, because when you're dead and gone, none of what you did in this life will matter.

Many people say they should have done something different and better with their lives, but now they're just too old. How old is too old? People return to college in their eighties. Inventors create incredible gadgets late in life. Artists and writers produce their finest work during their twilight years. Mother Teresa got a late start. She didn't begin to fulfill her destiny until she was in her forties. It wasn't easy. Her path was strewn with obstacles and nay-sayers. That's life.

When the going gets tough, the tough get going.

Doesn't matter if you're eighteen or eighty-eight, when you hear the voice, when you see the path, it's time to rise up and take action. Developing your personal brand demands courage. You may be scorned and ridiculed. You may be disowned by friends and family. They may not understand or approve of your purpose, but they're not responsible for your fate. That honor resides in you and you alone.

Mother Teresa is only one example. There are literally millions of people who achieved greatness late in life. Sometimes they are called "late bloomers," Most times we aren't even aware of their journey. We just join the story in progress and stand in amazement at what they are able to accomplish.

You are incredibly special and unique. You are the only flower in the species. Once you bloom and die, there will never be another like you. It's your choice. Whether your flower blooms in the middle of a jungle and is never seen or whether you are on the main float in the Rose Parade, you have a time, a place, and a purpose. Nobody grows, blooms, withers, and dies without consequence.

What should you do with your life? How should you live? Are you on the right track? Only you know the answers. Don't shake your head. Just because the answers aren't jumping out at you doesn't mean they're not in there. Even exceptional people who accomplish exceptional things struggle with these questions. The difference between them and people who never find their direction is effort. Mother Teresa didn't wake up one day with all the answers. It took a long time for her to find her purpose. She was troubled by the same doubts as you and me.

That's why attention to your personal brand is so important. If you don't separate yourself from the herd, you might as well be an eating and breathing machine. Going along just to get along stifles your unique qualities and abilities. Not living a values-centered life is a waste of your eternal soul, not to mention bad branding.

When you look deep and determine who you are and what your purpose is, it's impossible for anyone to deter you from your ultimate fate. Your personal brand was breathed into you at the moment of your conception (or maybe before). They broke the mold when you came into being. Your purpose, like Mother Teresa, might be to affect the lives of millions, or it might be to create hope for one poor downtrodden soul.

You may not know the final outcome. You may still not understand why you are the way you are, but you can strive to know yourself better each day. You can consciously work to know what you're supposed to do and be. It's your life. Your purpose is revealed in your dreams and spoken daily by your quiet inner voice.

Put yourself in an environment that fosters self-reflection. Surround yourself with people who are committed to helping you achieve your goals. Close your eyes and listen. When you find your calling, pursue it without regret. Be strong. You can change the world. Enjoy doing your thing, being the best that you can be.

Here's another way to express the journey toward originality. Metamorphosize—break out of your shell and spread your wings without concern. You may be surrounded by people who have no clue who you really are. They know your name and what you look like, but they refuse to accept you for you. Always remember that your purpose and direction are ultimately more important than their opinions.

The journey of brand development involves taking chances. When you arrive at your destiny, there may not be anybody standing to cheer you at the finish line. Many of the greatest people in history were rejected, ridiculed, and persecuted by their peers. Jesus was crucified. Keep your eyes on the prize. Discovering your brand carries with it many incredible rewards, but also the possibility of lost relationships. Admitting to yourself and to the world that you are someone quite different from the person they've come to know has the potential to shake some folks loose.

People who truly know you will accept you unconditionally. If you have the courage of your convictions and, like Mother Teresa, you are willing to make any sacrifice to accomplish your ultimate goal, fasten your seatbelt and prepare for lift-off.

19

Your Best You

Your best you isn't accomplished by chance. Like most things of value, if you want it, you have to work for it. Being lazy won't help you reach your destination. You'll have to consciously put effort into the task of re-connecting with the authentic you that may have been buried inside since you were a child. The first and most important step is to want to be all that you can be. If you're satisfied with what people have always told you about yourself, or the easy road that you've followed to this point, you won't find your authentic brand. Oliver North said it well, "An easy life is rarely meaningful, and a meaningful life is rarely easy."

Here are some basic principles necessary to become your best you. Slow down and pay attention to everything. And I mean everything. Your thoughts, your breath, your body, the clouds and stars in the sky, all the people and things around you—everything in your sphere.

Constantly check to see that your thoughts, words, actions and inactions are in sync with the image that you hold in your heart. Are you consumed by negative thoughts? Do you use language that doesn't accurately reflect the kind of person you are? Do you do things that you're ashamed of? Have you been afraid to do things that you know need doing? Do you neglect your health and well-being? Are you taking drugs that distort your reality? Are your friends stunting your spiritual growth? Do you have other bad habits? Smoking? Alcohol? Eating? Lack of exercise? What is it that holds you back? Are you ready to chuck all the negative influences in your life and embark on a determined and difficult journey?

There are many answers, but only one that suits you. The truth resonates within you. You know it like you know your own name. I've run into people who insist that they don't know who they are or what their purpose is. I tell them the same thing I'm telling you. Try harder. Look deeper. You've learned how to pretend. You can go through the motions with ease. You may have been doing it for years! Being completely authentic is easy too, but it takes practice and repetition and time. You may falter, but every human is capable of finding their best self.

When you analyze your relationships, are you satisfied that people close to you are holding you to the highest standards? In other words, do they contribute to your growth as a person? And finally, when you look in a mirror, is the person you're looking at deserving of your respect? Don't worry about comparing that person to anyone else in the world. There is no comparison. You're the only you. If you don't respect yourself, figure out why and fix the problem.

Commit to being honest and authentic. Don't expect or allow anyone or anything to direct you away from your goal. Always tell the truth, especially when it's difficult. The truth is a powerful ally.

Win friends and influence people through honest, authentic actions. Put honesty, truth, and personal values above the pursuit of wealth, power, or influence. People will trust you and seek your advice. Always put the best interest of others above your own selfish interests. Become the person you were meant to be.

Celebrate peace of mind every day. Be aware of everything in your world. Use your eyes, ears, and all your senses to experience the natural world. Base your decisions on real life experiences. Always seek truth. When you use technology, be cautious. Don't allow the web to suck you into the matrix. Never pretend to be someone you are not.

Be healthy, in mind, body and spirit. Consciously work to eliminate all the negatives in your life. Enjoy life, every minute of every day. Laugh. Greet people. Make eye contact. Smile. Forgive yourself when you make mistakes and fall short of your personal goals, but never quit trying to improve.

Be thoughtful, courteous and kind. When you're in a hurry, remind yourself to slow down. See yourself from a higher perspective. Know that you're never alone. Sync your thoughts, words and actions with the person you know you should and could be. Be awake, alert, and conscious of yourself in every respect. Surrender to the forces you can't control as you take total command of every personal decision.

Don't believe what you know is not true. Be aware when people are asking you to play a role, and politely but firmly show them who you are. Allow your brand to be visible and obvious to everyone you come in contact with. Be yourself, morning, noon and night.

Remember that being you is a beautiful thing. Avoid traps that lead you away from your goal of honesty and authenticity. Experience and share love. Offer a helping hand often and accept help when you are in need. Listen, reflect, meditate, remember and pray without reservation. Share the light with everyone you meet.

Thanks for reading, and don't hesitate to engage me (or anyone) in discussion about your personal brand.

Epilogue

I first left the monastery exactly forty days after I arrived. The abbot suggested that I should return to the outside world and try to find a job.

"If you don't find work," he said, "I have a project here and I could use your help. You are always welcome to come back." I was scared, but I packed my car and headed out.

As I got closer to the city, the first thing I noticed was how fast things were moving. There was traffic everywhere and people were in a hurry. It took serious concentration just to keep up.

In Dallas, I went right to work sending out resumes, making calls and setting up interviews. The first few days I lined up a half dozen meetings, and I was feeling optimistic. My first stop was the radio station I used to manage.

The new manager took me to lunch. I explained that I would take any job in the newsroom. I just needed a job, and I promised that I would be supportive of management and wouldn't cause any problems. He was polite, but he explained that I was far too overqualified and urged me to try something else.

Each stop after that I heard a version of the same theme, "You're just not a good fit for what we have. With your credentials I'm sure you'll find a better job."

Finally, I got a call from a private high school principal. He said he needed a development director, and that my credentials were perfect. The interview went great, and the next day he called to say I was his choice. Twists and turns. What a journey, I thought. After two weeks of frustration, I was about to begin a new chapter.

When I showed up on Monday to fill out paperwork, the principal had a strange look on his face as I walked into his office. "I'm so sorry," he began, "but I've been told I have to hire another candidate." I started to protest. After all, he had promised me the job. Sound familiar?

For two weeks I had done everything in my power to re-enter the world, but it wasn't my time. So, I listened to my quiet little voice, packed some clothes and returned to the monastery.

I already knew the routine, so it was easy to settle in. My assignments were clear, and I moved through the next six months with few distractions. During that period many people came to the monastery for retreats. Some were going through personal tragedies, some were lost, and some were just there to recharge their spiritual batteries. Observing their behavior gave me a fresh perspective. I saw how the monks' quiet presence affected visitors. It's hard to describe, but somehow just being in that special environment created a healing effect. Everyone was touched by the peace they found there.

When I finally left the monastery after more than seven months of monastic living, I had no idea where I was going, but I wasn't frightened in the least. It was a completely different experience. I felt calm and confident. "Things will work out," I told myself. And I was right.

My post-monastic life is filled with adventures. I have had some great jobs, made many new friends and I learn new things about myself every day. I've written two books about decisions and have been blessed to share my thoughts about personal branding with wonderful audiences across the country.

Life never unfolds in a straight line. There's no way of knowing what might happen later today, much less tomorrow or next week. Don't waste a minute, and never take anything for granted.

Every moment of every day, be grateful that you are exactly where you're intended to be, even when you don't know where you are or how you got there. Everything in your life is part of an eternal blueprint based on the decisions you make each day. Choose wisely.

Being angry and upset is a waste of time. There's no point in trying to force things. Being our best means being prepared for whatever comes our way.

Learning who we are doesn't happen without purposeful reflection. Being authentic is harder than it looks, but not so hard as to discourage anyone who wants to try.

The journey is littered with signs and little miracles. Learn to pay attention to the signs. They are everywhere. Be grateful for the miracles. Don't judge. Just read the signs and follow your path.

When one door closes, even if it slams in your face, slide past and look for open doors. When you're sad or depressed, remember a happy time and move to recapture that feeling.

You don't need a monastic experience to start fresh. Keep your tool chest stocked with prayer, meditation, listening and remembering. The more time you spend with your tools, the easier it is to deal with life's challenges and disappointments.

Wishing you peace, quiet, happiness, health and a fun-filled journey toward finding your personal brand and being you again.

Acknowledgements

With gratitude and special thanks to John Leonard. Patient coach, advisor, critic, and friend, John transforms my thoughts into images and pushes me to be a better writer and a better person.

To Dan Crissman, the world's finest editor. Dan's empathy for his clients allows him to understand what we mean even when we struggle to express it properly. His thoughtful criticism enhances every word, sentence and paragraph.

To my new friend Jack LeMenager who applied his talent to the text as well, managing and organizing thoughts into a more readable format.

To sons Casey and Brock for helping me work through some generational language issues in this manuscript. Their gentle yet direct critiques pushed me to refine and clarify my thoughts.

To friends and family, but especially to strangers who continue to support my writing. It's impossible to sufficiently express my gratitude for your thoughtful feedback. Our common goal is to raise collective consciousness. Your reviews and correspondence are inspiring.

And to God for my many blessings, challenges, successes and failures. I am committed to making my life a reflection of His eternal goodness.

About The Author

Charlie Seraphin is an observer of American culture. As a news reporter, radio news anchor, news director, general manager, senior vice president and professor, he's covered many of the important issues of our lifetime. He's met and interviewed decision makers that contributed to the stories that shape our world, always striving to report details in a fair and balanced manner.

In his first book, *One Stupid Mistake*, Charlie set out to explore the complexities of decision-making. He queried hundreds of people about their successes and failures. He is a great listener and meticulous observer. He asks probing questions in search of the truth.

While many reporters are focused on macro issues and global politics, Charlie has come to understand that every story begins with an individual decision. What we do, or what we fail to do determines outcomes. How we think, speak, act and fail to act are all reflected in the world around us. People make things happen.

From his early days as a news reporter, Charlie consciously distilled stories into words that everyone can understand. Radio news doesn't work without painted word pictures. He uses plain language and a relatively simple formula. Be fair and respectful. Don't inject opinions unless they're labeled as opinions. Tell memorable stories.

Because voice, tone, choice of words, and many other factors inject themselves into communication, it would be foolish to believe in pure objectivity, in journalism or anywhere else. We are all biased based on our environment, background and experiences. Charlie's work is no exception. You'll know where he's coming from and where he stands. But he allows each reader to pursue their individual course of action.

What makes us do the things we do? Why is it so difficult to accept responsibility for what we've done? Heavy stuff, but readers are pleasantly surprised by his wit, humor and common sense. Charlie takes serious subjects and makes them fun and easy to understand.

His thought-provoking books challenge us to ask questions, of ourselves and of others. He believes we're all reporters. We're all seeking truth. Charlie Seraphin's books aren't intended to provide answers. Instead they help us formulate our own questions so that all of our decisions are better informed.

Made in the USA
Monee, IL
13 September 2021